A HAPPY JOURNEY
STORIES FROM THE HEART

By Larry Welch

Order this book online at www.trafford.com
or email orders@trafford.com

Most Trafford titles are also available at major online book retailers.

Printed in the United States of America.

ISBN: 978-1-4269-5179-4 (sc)
ISBN: 978-1-4269-5271-5 (e)

Trafford rev. 02/28/2011

www.trafford.com

North America & International
toll-free: 1 888 232 4444 (USA & Canada)
phone: 250 383 6864 ♦ fax: 812 355 4082

For my loving sister,
Linda Kay Freshour,
No days pass that her warm spirit
doesn't brighten life's path

What people are saying...

Within seconds of meeting Larry Welch, you cannot help but realize that you are in the presence of somebody extraordinary. Larry is an influence of positivity wherever he goes, caring for and loving people deeply. He radiates warmth and light from within. I have been the recipient of his monthly electronic newsletter "On the run..." for many years and am delighted to see that he has put these 53 vignettes together in "A Happy Journey." This book promises to be delightfully refreshing, touching, heartwarming and, I dare say, healing to the soul. Observe the world through the eyes of Larry and may you be awakened to a new reality – one that is indeed beautiful, magnificent and magical. We could all do with a little Larry in our lives. I cannot recommend this book highly enough. May you relish every word as did I. Dr. Martha Lee, Clinical Sexologist of Eros Coaching, Singapore

Larry has done it again! The secret to his writings is one part travel-log, a half-part geography lesson, another half-part history discourse, some common sense sprinkled in, and a splash of silent humor all mixed with a special ingredient - people around the world with the same concerns, issues or needs. Most of his stories have a moral; some are clear, but some stories challenge the reader to interpret and conclude the meaning or message. Ralph Compton, retired engineer, Virginia Beach, Virginia

Larry Welch's "A Happy Journey" recounts stories of the many people he has met in his travels. I being one of those he has met, I found the book inspiring, intimate and human. Larry's' altruistic manner and general likability put all who encounter him at ease allowing the story to emerge. His years of travel have taken him to places off the beaten path that even the well worn traveler can appreciate. The stories he shares are all around us, they are in everyone we meet and interact with. Larry's true gift isn't the great friend he is or the fine example of an American that he is but rather the storyteller, traveler and humanist. Enjoy "A Happy Journey", see the world thru Larry's eyes and meet the people that he has met. Captain Kurt Hummeldorf, DC, USN, Manassas, Virginia

I have followed Larry's adventures in his "On the run . . ." newsletter for many years. Through it I have become more and more aware, not only of his unique qualities and multitude of interests, but also of the rich, multi-cultural world in which we live. Larry's vignettes, in which he lovingly and humorously exposes us to the details of life in a variety of cultural settings, and in which he emphasizes the basic goodness of the great majority of the people he has met, are mind-expanding. One comes away feeling a little bit better about the world and its problems, with the realization that "yes, it IS possible, at least at times, for human beings to live in harmony." The gamut of situations described in "A Happy Journey" is wide, each story is detailed, and not infrequently the change in ambiance from one story to the next is pronounced. Larry's love of writing and his love of people shine through these stories. He has no doubt worked for years to develop this expertise, but develop it he has, to the point where he skillfully prepares the reader with succinct, well-researched background information, and rapidly transitions to an astonishingly detailed and intimate glimpse of the people with whom he has interacted. With each story the reader is drawn into a new and perhaps strange new world, and is unable to resist reading through to the end. I am reminded of a string of precious stones, each with its own unique sparkle and color. In "A Happy Journey" Larry Welch offers us a new and positive perspective on life. I sincerely wish that I had his ability to touch our hearts, and I highly recommend the book to those who would expand their horizons in this small way. Fred Ferate, Austin, Texas

Larry's book is provocative and captivating reading. He has an unusual power of observation, a love for all people, and an enthusiasm for adventure. His honest and refreshing way with words opens up to the reader stories that are "from the heart". Larry embraces life. His stories bring you the unforgettable people he has met in faraway places. The reader is challenged to share in his experiences. I found the stories to be thought provoking and from a historical point of view extremely interesting. Jacqueline Delaverdac DeMent, Kalamazoo, Michigan

About the Author

Larry Welch resides in Thailand where he operates the Full Moon Rubber Plantation at Nakhon Phanom and was until recently an English teacher at the Suankularb Wittayalai Rangsit School in a suburb north of Bangkok. In his day-to-day routine he taught English to 600 students in grades 7, 10 and 11. Although only a second year teacher, it is his belief that it's impossible to have a bad day when surrounded by that much good-natured humanity.

In 1995 and again in 1999, he was selected as Toastmaster of the Year for the District of Columbia, Northern Virginia and Southern Maryland. In 1996, he became the first recipient of the National Race for the Cure Volunteer of the Year Award; and he was presented the 1997 Jill Ireland Award for Voluntarism by The Susan G. Komen Breast Cancer Foundation in Dallas, Texas. In 1998 and again in 2002, the Naval Criminal Investigative Service presented him with a Department of the Navy Meritorious Civilian Service Award for his leadership in community service and contributions to the agency mission. Toastmasters International has also recognized him as their Club President of the Year and Division Governor of the Year. In 2009, he received a Model Teacher Award from the Pathumthani Provincial Minister of Education.

An avid reader and learner, in 1995, he earned a Bachelor of Science degree (management) from University College, University of Maryland, after attending night school for nine years.

In 1984, he retired from the Navy as a Lieutenant (Limited Duty-Cryptology). Before a second retirement from the US Naval Criminal Investigative Service in 2007, he was employed as a civilian security specialist in Singapore performing vulnerability assessments at seaports and airfields in Asia and the South Pacific.

An inquisitive and energetic traveler, Larry has worked, lived, or traveled to 40 countries.

For the past 12 years he has authored the electronic newsletter, *On the run...*, which reflects a street-smart philosophy on the places he visits and people he meets-- along with ideas on how we can be our best.

He is author of *Mary Virginia, A Father's Story*; *Quotations for Positive People, And Those Who Would Like to Be*; and *The Human Spirit, Stories from the Heart*.

Larry can be reached by e-mail at lnwelch@aol.com or lnwelch@hotmail.com.

Prologue

The 53 vignettes in *A Happy Journey* first appeared in *On the run...* during 2004-08. I wrote the stories to capture my experiences as an expatriate living in Singapore and Thailand while traveling to many other locales.

The stories are reproduced in book form to provide a collection of thoughts for readers of today's *On the run...* as well as to be a permanent reference for my family, friends, and new readers.

The stories are about real people that seem a degree removed from the ordinary. They interested me not just because they were part of my own journey, but the experiences taught me the rich diversity of our humanity. People laugh and cry around the world, the things that touch these emotions differ from place to place. Entertaining ghosts, riding camels, and getting married in the Maldives are part and parcel of our world, but not your everyday experience. Some of the stories hint at exotic surroundings not found anywhere else in the world, other stories contain historical records so obscure they don't qualify as even footnotes to our human experience, and lastly, the reader will see that regardless of our skin color, religion, or economic circumstances, we are all brothers and sisters in a large human family.

In 2007, the world lost three angels that I knew personally: Americans Bobbie Culp and Rosemary Williams; and Thailand's Noun Bootiem. It isn't easy saying goodbye to those we love, respect, and find unforgettable. I included them in the book as a lasting tribute to three better than excellent people who I will not forget.

The book reflects my beliefs and a love for our natural world, human nature, and Christianity. I think that people of the Islamic, Buddhist, and Hindu faiths are every bit as devote, kind, and generous as we Christians. That respectful view comes from first-hand experience through friendship with people in many countries. *A Happy Journey* is also about faith, gratitude, and optimism. America has been good to me from the start with a secure and loving family, educational opportunities galore, steadfast friends, and the chance to serve others. A sense of gratitude is in my heart, thoughts and words.

All of us are struggling with one thing or another, no one's life is a bowl of cherries. I hope that *A Happy Journey* will inspire you to a new and more positive view of our magnificent world.

Table of Contents

2004

2005

2006

2007

2008

2004

Keeping Life in Perspective

For the past several weeks I've been on travel to Brunei and Indonesia. These are good places to find surprises, learn a little more about the world, and have at least one adventure around every corner.

Waiting for my flight to Brunei at Singapore's Changi Airport, I was having coffee when Mary Fitzpatrick, an attractive woman from Hong Kong, asked if she could sit at my table. It's not common that pretty young women ask to share my table. Of course, I was flattered until I realized that my table was the only spot with an empty seat. Be that as it may, it was nice to meet Mary, an Asian sales representative for Elekta Medical Systems. In our chitchat over one thing and another we discovered a common interest in Vietnam where we found a shared experience in both having had gold chains stolen from around our necks. Mary's was grabbed while she was riding on the back of a motorcycle; mine was snatched while jogging on a busy street at 7 am. Funny thing, my chain was a good luck charm, now it's bringing someone else good fortune! But my luck actually improved without the charm. I met Mary didn't I?

While jogging beside a road in Brunei's capital city of Bandar Seri Begawan early one morning, a lady named Bev stopped her car and rolled down her car window to say hello. As I approached her car, she asked three questions: *Do you speak*

English? Can you drive a car? Will you drive me home? A pretty blond with an English accent, I thought how fortunate I was to attract such a lovely woman. Then she explained that she was having an anxiety attack and would appreciate it if I could help her get home. Yes, her hands were shaking badly and her voice quivering. Bev and her husband had been living in Brunei for six years and were now planning on returning to the Yorkshires of England, but she wasn't happy about it. Although I hadn't driven a car in nearly a year, Bev got home okay.

Bandar Seri Begawan has one of the largest water villages in the world. Situated at Kampong Ayer there is actually a collection of 28 water villages with thousands of homes, schools, hospitals, mosques, fire departments, and stores that sit on stilts on the river. One afternoon I took a boat ride through the village. The boat coxswain, an amiable young man, kept up an energetic description of the buildings and lifestyle of the residents. He even took us past his home so we could wave to his grandmother.

We passed schools where kids went out of their way to smile and wave; adults did the same from their verandahs. It was the kind of warm, friendly community where you truly felt welcome. As we passed one little boy, a 4-5 year old, I gave him my best wave. He gave me the one finger salute! Well, no one place in the world is perfect.

A few mornings later I was jogging on Darmo Raya, a nice street at Surabaya, Indonesia; thousands of people passed on motorbikes and bicycles en route to small businesses, school and work. Merchants with their carts piled high with assorted fresh vegetables and fruits were pushing, pulling and pedaling their way up the street where a gathering of neighborhood women waited. There were also a few other joggers. They were running in their bare feet; women in dresses, men in shorts and t-shirts. I was also wearing clothes. Then there was the naked man. He had no clothes and there were none in sight. He was walking, had an innocent expression, and not much to hide. Later at the hotel, I asked one of the female desk

14

clerks about the naked man, she wouldn't comment until she'd summoned her woman coworkers so I could repeat the naked man story. They giggled, then all nodded in agreement that the guy was nuts.

While at Surabaya, I stayed at the Shangri-La Hotel, a lovely home away from home. I noticed that they had a sign in the lobby that bans durian. That's a good thing. Durian is a tropical fruit that smells worse than a dead skunk, the tree it grows on also stinks. I had never seen a hotel ban durians, but I'd like to put a sign like that up outside my home in Singapore. I tried durian once, a Thai friend, Nisa Wichitsiri, brought it as an introduction to local culture. It smelled up the house so bad we had to open windows and doors for several hours. The odor gets on your clothes, too. Interesting thing, half of Asians are smart like me and don't like to be around durian; the other half thinks it's a great treat.

If there is a common theme to these vignettes it may be that it's helpful to not take life too seriously. Losing something material like a gold chain isn't the end of the world, keeping your sense of humor through unexpected everyday events makes for great fun, and banning durian is a good idea.

Monkey Shines at Kuantan

Recently it was my good fortune to spend two weeks in the lush green landscape of Malaysia visiting the communities of Tioman Island, Penang, Langkawi, and Kuantan. This time around I experienced a special hug, watched meaningful handholding, and hosted a monkey party.

Malaysia is a moderate Muslim country of 23 million people who have worked hard over the past several generations to lift their country into a land of prosperity. They manufacture textiles, electronics and their own automobile, the Proton. The Proton operates on both gasoline and propane for fuel economy. The country is not poor, but not rich. It resides somewhere in the perfect place between where people are pleased with prospects for the future, but not so materialistic it has driven them away from their traditional values. Their per capital income is about $9,300 (vs. $24,000 in Singapore or $3,100 in neighboring Indonesia). The country has a diverse cultural, ethnic and religious population of Chinese, Indians, and Malays who practice Islam, Buddhism, Hindu, and Christianity. There has been so much intermarriage that one can scarcely criticize ethnicity or religion without insulting a relative and English was selected as a neutral language so that no one could claim their language is best. The country has a British colonial history, which adds an interesting ingredient to architecture, laws and many of the customs. Features that I like are that most of the country is covered in rain forest, it is green everywhere, there are jungle creatures, and the beaches are fabulous.

Tioman Island is 18 miles from the Malaysian mainland and not far from Signapore. In the 1970s, *Time* magazine declared Tioman one of the ten most beautiful islands in the world. It has 3,000 residents and more stars in the sky than most parts of the world. Well, I suppose we all have the same number of stars, it's just that you can see them better at Tioman because they don't have light pollution. Three thousand people don't generate that much light plus there are less than four miles of paved roadway.

Besides the amazing display of stars spied on my early morning jog, I chanced upon a large group of monitor lizards that were in the 3-4 foot range. They were swimming in a canal; nearby was a large family of long-tailed macaque monkeys dining on leftovers at a restaurant.

It was also at Tioman that I watched a mother and son hold hands. The 5-year old was a Down's syndrome child whose mother had brought him to the resort lobby to learn about the long list of recreation activities. Parents and kids holding hands are powerful moments. It says everything is okay and that generally seems to be good enough.

Later in my travels at the resort island of Langkawi I was at the international airport. I visited the gift shop, where a young woman passed who was wearing the right perfume. She strolled by a second time and that was what did it for me. I introduced myself, told her I liked the perfume and asked about the fragrance. Ogi Demchig was her name and she waltzed me next door to the perfume store to show me the brand. One thing led to another, Ogi told me she was an attorney from Mongolia, but now working as a computer consultant at Perth, Australia. She was on her way to Israel to visit a girlfriend who was marrying a Frenchman. I love these international relationships. At any rate, every 10-12 years, I meet a stranger, know them for five minutes, and they want to hug. Ogi's flight was called, she hugged, and I did my gentlemanly duty to be equally as affectionate. Ogi gave me a lesson about the high quality of people that are populating the earth. The perfume was Treson from Lancôme.

Penang, another island, was the next stop on my itinerary. Penang was one of the three trading posts along with Singapore and Melaka to be administered by the British East India Company on the Straits of Malacca. It is a beautiful island dominated by the colonial city of Georgetown, which has a traditional Chinatown community, the sort one might find 50 years in the past.

One evening workmates and I visited the Eden Seafood Village, a theater-style restaurant. The menu is supported by 36 tanks for fresh fish, squirming eels, and other urchins of the sea; and the stage is complete with young entertainers who demonstrate Malaysia's folk artistry through traditional song and dance. As impressive as it all was a 12-year old girl captured my attention for her courage and determination. She arrived with her parents and together they walked hand-in-hand to a nearby table. The little girl's legs were deformed; her walk was an awkward up and down and sideways motion. It was both sad and inspiring to see one so young afflicted and to know the suffering that she has endured with no choice but to be brave, trust her loving parents, and keep faith in the future. This little girl and the Down's syndrome boy at Tioman remind us that some people wear their halos better than others.

They brief guests at Kuantan's Hyatt Regency Hotel to keep their balcony doors shut, but I missed the point. Kuantan is a city on the southeast coast of Malaysia, not too far from Tioman and Singapore. It is a small community of 150,000 people and has just one 5-star hotel, The Hyatt. The hotel is sited on a pretty beach with rainforest as a back drop. The forest is filled with hordes of monkeys who have smartly learned over the years that their human cousins at the Hyatt will give them a hand-out. Remember the instructions I didn't get about leaving balcony doors shut?

One evening, with my balcony doors open, I left the room for about an hour. When I returned a monkey was sitting on the balcony waiting for me. I named him Cody. Cody wanted peanuts so I went to the mini-bar and got him peanuts. Then his brother Scooter arrived, he wanted peanuts, too. Elvis came swinging down from the balcony above, I wanted to give him fruit and that's when I noticed that the monkeys had already visited my room and taken my stash of bananas. He didn't seem to mind getting potato chips. Peggy Sue arrived; she was shy, but wanted chips, too. I fulfilled her wish. As they finished their snacks, they wandered off...then Mike, a squirrel, arrived but there were no more snacks. He had to be disappointed but didn't show it—even squirrels can be positive in their outlook. He simply turned around and headed for greener pastures.

And so it goes in Malaysia with the clasping of hands, halos, hugs, and monkey shines...good experiences and good memories. I am glad I could be there.

Amazing Grace

Amazing Grace, how sweet the sound that saved a wretch like me! I once was lost, but now am found, was blind, but now I see.

I love the song *Amazing Grace*. Many people do. For the past several weeks I've been thinking of the words in that old hymn, reading about grace in M. Scott Peck's book *The Road Less Traveled* and watching people nurture human life and spiritual growth.

It started a month ago with a one-week working vacation at Phuket, Thailand. This is the first time I have used the words working and vacation in the same sentence; they don't harmonize except when you're thinking about having your agency send you on assignment to a paradise.

Thailand is known as the Land of Smiles and for good reason. People walk around with a happy face. In what was once known as Siam, the gesture of a smile is made before a verbal greeting. I like that and suspect that most of you would enjoy the experience as well.

While at Phuket I worked, but also spent time with the Techo family. I've know the matriarch, Wanvisa, for a year. Wan has grace. She is a university-educated economist who understands business. Besides working 7-days a week at her restaurant, she manages a farm with cattle, commercial fish ponds, and chickens; and heads her immediate family of two kids, and a younger sister and brother. Wanvisa is hardworking and a source of gentle encouragement for her family and customers. Everyone respects and likes her. She recently went to a Buddhist Monastery near Bangkok for ten days to help the monks and to learn more about her religion. There were 1,100 other volunteer women there. They wore simple white dresses, arose at 4:30 am, then cleaned, cooked, and studied until 9:30 pm. It was 10-days of grace.

Three weeks ago, I spent a week with the Toluang family at Ban Khok Kloi, a small town on Thailand's west coast. This really was a vacation. I rode elephants, went boating, watched monkey shines, read books, went to bed early-slept late, and jogged in splashes of colorful sunrises and sunsets.

The best of everything was being with the Toluang family. They are Muslim and also own a restaurant. The extended family is mom and dad, two daughters, a son, a son-in-law, sister-in-law, and three grandchildren. They have grace. Particularly remarkable was the way they patiently nurture small children and the love they possess for those around them—even a foreigner like me. Grace shows in the eyes, the gestures, and a touch. Watching this family live simply, yet with richness of character was an education in Life 101.

Living better with less should be a priority, but we most often find ourselves caught in lockstep with a world that counts material possession as the ultimate mark of distinction. On May 4, Supaporn Toluang, one of the daughters, celebrated her 28th birthday. As part of her special day, she let me tag along as she donated a car truck filled with snacks to an orphanage for special needs children.   Not everyone things about their birthday as being a good day to do something nice for others. It was a lesson for me.

Two weeks ago, I was the Singapore host for Tran Thi Mong Chinh, a 29-year old university graduate from Vietnam. She was on her first vacation. Chinh inspires. Now manager of the CC Fashion Store in Saigon, she started working nights and weekends when she was ten. Recently she took her life savings, $3,500, and gave it to her parents so that they could repair and remodel their home.   Saving that much money in the Vietnamese economy is no small feat.   Even as a college graduate, her salary is only 50 cents an hour. Chinh is Catholic, her father was a helicopter mechanic for the US military, and her English is excellent. So is her character. In recounting for me her family history, experiences in education and business, and voluntarism in her community, I learned more about devotion to spirituality, nurturing of children even when they aren't yours, and dedication to family.

Sometimes grace lives in a memory. Chelsea Cromartie's grace lives in the heart of those in her family. On May 3, Chelsea was killed in Washington, DC. She was eight. All of us have grace, most especially our children. They are carbon copies of us, only without the bad habits. Chelsea was killed while watching television in her aunt's living room. A stray bullet tore through the front window hitting her in the head. It was an accident, the anonymous shooter was aiming for someone else, and we don't know who because he hasn't been caught. I didn't know Chelsea, but it's certain that the world can scarcely afford to lose another angel. Condolences go out to Martha Morant, Chelsea's grandmother.

I'd like to know more about grace and I am learning. My sense of it is that acquiring grace is a conscientious lifetime effort. We stop, look and listen to those around us and do our best to keep faith, hope and charity. Our classroom is everyday situations and the teachers can be anyone we meet. Everyone has something good to share including grace.

State of Disappointment

Several weeks ago, I was in a state of disappointment. We all have those times when things don't turn out as planned. These occasions can be used as opportunities or something less. When I had two business trips cancelled back-to-back, I grimaced and wondered how I'd happily survive sitting in one place for three weeks. Rolling the options over in my mind, I knew there had to be a reasonably good constructive use of the time.

Although unglamorous, the thought came to mind that I could flex my mental muscle on projects that I'd been putting off. I wavered with the thoughts of how flabby my mental muscle happens to be, but gradually the idea of getting caught up on some overdue projects captured my imagination. And that's how I came to be probed, pricked and pinched at Mount Elizabeth's Hospital in Singapore. It was all part of my annual physical that had been deferred for five years. Shame on me!

My poor example notwithstanding, getting an annual physical is the right kind of thinking. If you have time or not, good health should not be taken for granted. In fact, if you abuse tobacco, alcohol, food, or drugs, it's probably a good idea to visit the doctor every six months, but don't expect your insurance company to understand. As our bodies age, there are too many things that can go wrong. It seems we are custodians of a complex living organism that exists in a delicate balance of chemistry. When an imbalance occurs things can go terribly wrong in relatively short order.

In my case, I am too intimate with food, not all foods, of course, just those best taken in moderation. My favorites are fried chicken, fried rice, fried noodles, cheeseburgers, French fries, chocolate, fruit pies, ice cream, cheese, and peanut butter.

I don't like any of these foods in moderation or as an occasional treat.

During my physical I excelled on the stress test, chest x-ray, CT scan, blood pressure readings, and blood chemistry; but not all the blood chemistry. The cholesterol reading was out of whack. My doctor, Robert Don, is a prince. He is older and smarter than the norm and I knew he could have given me a strict lecture on the benefits of living a more healthy life. Before he did that I assured him that I was knowledgeable about good eating practices. We all know what proper dietary habits are, but a great many of us fail to practice them, especially Americans, Canadians, Australians and those from Western Europe. That's why there are so many heavyweights in those parts of the world.

Asians are generally slim, but they are buying more spandex and clothes with elastic waistbands these days. That's because of the import of Western culture. Let's try to count the ways: Burger King, McDonald's, KFC, Pizza Hut, California Pizza, Mrs. Fields, Famous Amos, Swenson's Ice Cream, Dunkin' Donuts, Dairy Queen, Haagen Dazs and Baskin and Robbins. All these restaurants and shops are located within four blocks of my home in Singapore and they are popular. We become a double threat to ourselves when we procrastinate on eating properly and then put off the bad news by not getting a physical. Doesn't make much sense, does it?

But wait there's more. My procrastination list is a lengthy one. There was the last will and testament put off for 15-years, completion of a book review started 4 months earlier, a deferred appointment with the dentist delayed 2-years, resumption of work on a book after 3-months of inactivity, registration for absentee voting put off since January, and a postponed vigor in getting the Social Security Administration to correct my birthday that they arbitrarily changed 10-years ago.

None of these things are important to anyone except me, which may be the point. We rush through life caring for everyone and everything except that character we live with day-in and day-out, ourselves. The past few weeks were positive and productive as I'd planned, but more than that I've learned to slow down and give more deliberate thought to priorities that don't matter much to anyone except me.

Aussies and their Neighbors

Life is a busy place for all of us; it often seems there is precious little time to do the important things that need doing. I recently returned from three weeks business travel to Fiji, Tonga, and Australia. The trip allowed me to escape the drum beat of housecleaning, laundry, making my bed and those sort of *things that need doing.*

During the three weeks I flew thousands of miles, slept in nine hotels, attended countless business meetings and socials, jogged nearly 150 miles, and met at least a hundred interesting people. Because of all this I was changed for the better as open-minded travelers are apt to be. A few days ago, one of my workmates told me that no one has a better life than I do. I agree.

Travels took me to Lautoka and Suva, Fiji; Nuku'alofa, Tonga; and Sydney, Cairns, Melbourne, Brisbane, and Townsville, Australia. I am still in awe of the sweeping beauty of our world.

Lautoka and Suva are home to Polynesians, Indians, and tourists coming from America, Australia and Japan. Fiji is also the home of Vijay Singh, world famous golfer. The islands there have pretty beaches, colorful coral formations, sugar cane plantations, and kava.

Kava looks like dishwater and tastes the same. You can drink it hot or cold; it numbs the tongue, turns lips blue and relaxes jittery constitutions. Fijians like it a lot, so do the people at Tonga, that's where Nuku'alofa is. Tonga is a Polynesian kingdom with 100,000 people. But not everyone is Polynesian; I met immigrants from Australia, Italy, and Germany. They are artists, entrepreneurs, and pizza makers. The country has lovely sunsets, pretty beaches, and more churches per capita than any other country in the world. Those are distinctions we can live with. The country's leader is Tauofa'ahau Topou IV, he's the king.

The king holds the *Guinness Book of Records* for being the world's heaviest monarch. As a young man he weighed 450 pounds. Now 86, his birthday is July 4, he has reduced his girth to a slimmer 350 pounds through diet and exercise. Even at 86 the king likes to continue that exercise with bike riding, a matter of concern for his family. That's why soldiers run beside him when he bicycles, just to catch him if he falls. Not to be disrespectful, but I wonder if another soldier runs along with a bicycle pump to keep the tires inflated.

Fiji, Tonga and Australia are friendly neighboring countries; they are all located in the South Pacific. It's also the Southern Hemisphere and that's why its winter there, while the other half of the world is experiencing summer. In Australia, I asked several people how they coped without snow at Christmas. They politely responded with a smile that they got along just fine, thank you.

Sydney is the world's best city, that's what 425,105 readers of *Travel and Leisure* magazine said in their latest poll. It's not the first time Sydney has come in first. It has a magnificent harbor, art museums, and exquisite churches with old-fashioned tall steeples, an absorbing history, beautiful botanical gardens with thousands of flying foxes, generous treescapes, old European architecture, attractive people, and a concerned citizenry.

Not everything is good in Australia. They have pay toilets. A few other countries have the same thing, but they also have attendants that will let you in when you're broke. In Sydney, the toilet doors are coin operated without an attendant so that the most urgent calls of nature are unheard. There should be a United Nations regulation against pay toilets.

They also have magpies. Early one morning I was jogging on a Sydney street and a magpie bonked me in the back of the head. They are an aggressive and noisy bird that should be relocated to a part of the world uninhabited by humans. The pay toilets could go with them.

Australians are good friends to Americans and that bothers a few people—they think we're too cozy at times and that is sometimes part of the political debate there.

I attended four meetings of Toastmasters International (a nonprofit educational organization, which provides educational experiences in speaking, effective listening, critical thinking and leadership) in Australia and found that they like to make fun of Americans as much as I like to tease them. I also ate kangaroo in a tasty stew. Australians think it's good to eat kangaroos as they can be a bit pesky. Outsiders see them as a friendly, cute, and an unusually shaped animal that deserves better. I don't think we should eat cats, dogs, monkeys, or horses either, but people do.

Best jab of the trip came from Shane Wykes in Sydney. Shane works for the Royal Australian Navy Naval Investigative Service, my counterpart agency in the American Navy. When asked if he'd watched "NCIS," a TV program loosely based on my organization, Shane replied, *Yes, of course, it comes on here Sunday nights. I watched the first episode, fell asleep and never watched it again. Sorry mate!* It doesn't take much to make me laugh; I took his jab in good spirits.

If you're planning to visit Australia, apply for extra credit cards and bring lots of cash. In Melbourne, I started to turn my dirty clothes into the hotel laundry. Then I saw the prices: trousers $14, shirts $10, underwear $5. My practical side surfaced, I saved a ton of money and learned that you can wear a pair of pants more than once. Australia has a strong middle class and I like the way the country shares. Restaurants, taxis, clothes, and hotels are expensive, but the money goes to benefit people in a free economic environment. I saw an ad for an experienced waitress; the beginning wage was $17 an hour. People don't tip much.

Every city in Australia provided an enormously rich jogging environment with inspiring paths that invariably followed rivers, beaches, or harbors. The same was true for Fiji and Tonga. Lots of people run, especially in Australia. In the big cities the people aren't as friendly as they are in the smaller communities. That seems to be a universal truth all around the world. I also noticed Australian joggers run faster than I do. They made me feel bad. If there were speed limits for joggers, maybe set at 5.5 miles an hour, that wouldn't happen. We'd all run harmoniously along at about the same speed, we could chat, and laugh together. Of course, I could try to run faster, but then I wouldn't feel like laughing.

We all have an internal journal where we unconsciously jot down the good times we've had in life. Later, we recount the entries from our personal journal in gatherings of friends and family. Now you know not only how I used my time during the past several weeks, what the journal entries say, and what I'll be talking about for the next few weeks.

Sandakan Brothel No. 8

Running beside Labuk Road one evening I passed some boys just leaving soccer practice. They had on their team jerseys and were filled with life. I remember them for their smiles and because they all wanted to "high five" me as I ran past. Meeting kids who want to "high five" doesn't happen often, when it does, it's an honor.

Labuk Road is in a hilly suburb just outside the community of Sandakan, Malaysia, on the island of Borneo. The local area is colorful with lush jungle, pythons, wild boars, crocodiles, orangutans and proboscis monkeys, beaches, sea turtles, and tropical birds. The orangutans have long red hair, they are big, and only reside on Borneo and the nearby island of Sumatra (Indonesia). There's also an adventurous local history filled with pirates, headhunters, and Sandakan Brothel No. 8.

The brothel was run by a Japanese madam, Inoshita Okuni, who had first visited Singapore before moving to Sandakan to apply her trade. Okuni was known across the South Seas for her remarkable kindness and charity to people from all walks of life. She was probably known for other things, too, but being remembered for kindness is the epitome of where we should all want to be. A book and Japanese movie were made of her life.

Japanese girls and women forced into employment in brothels are referred to as karayuki-san. It is a sad commentary on history that a century ago Japan's three major exports were silk, coal and young women. As Japanese business interests expanded in Southeast Asia, homeland girls were sent to take care of another sort of business. Sandakan Brothel No. 8 was one of hundreds of establishments that catered to men with enslaved Japanese women. Today's term for the same practice is human trafficking.

The Sandakan area suffered horribly during World War II and several prisoner of war camps housed captured Europeans and Australians including American writer Agnes Keith (1901-82).

Keith was a grand storyteller who wrote about her life in the books: *Land Below the Wind, Three Came Home, White Man Returns,* and four other books. Each of her books makes captivating reading, one of which, *Three Came Home*, was made into a major motion picture.

Married to an English forest ranger, Harry Keith; she, her husband and young son spent three years in a Japanese POW camp on Borneo.

The record of one Japanese POW camp takes your breath when you learn that only 6 of 2,400 Australian patriots survived on reduced rations and forced marches.

It was a great privilege to visit Newlands, also known as the Agnes Keith home. It is surrounded by jungle on a high hill overlooking the picturesque harbor at Sandakan. On one delightful evening my traveling colleague, Kevin Wagoner, and I sat at a table on the grounds at Newlands, sipped tea, took in the panoramic view, felt the refreshing tropic breeze and talked about Agnes Keith. I think she would have been pleased.

Almost everywhere you go there is an interesting history worth digging up and once known the little part of the world you're occupying becomes more alive. You also realize how important it is to live the best and most healthy life you can out of respect for those who were robbed of their own time on earth.

Marriage and Divorce in the Maldives

Last week I visited the Maldives, a chain of islands in the Indian Ocean. The country has 270,000 people living on 200 islands. They are 100 percent Sunni Muslim. Many years ago they were under the rule of a sultan and when he converted to Islam so did all of his subjects.

Maldives is famed for fishing and European tourism. The tourists love diving in the clear aquamarine, turquoise and deep blue waters with colorful coral and tropical fish. On the islands, I enjoyed the thousands of parakeets that chirp shrilly. I couldn't tell if they were trying to communicate with each other or just singing for the fun of making a racket.

The Maldives has the highest divorce rate of any country in the world. It's that way because to get a divorce, all a man has to say to his wife is, *I am divorcing you*, and it's over. My guide book said that it wasn't unusual for someone to be divorced 10-20 times in their lifetime. The divorce record, 89, is held by a man in Male, the capital.

While visiting the Maldives Transport and Contract Company, I met a bright receptionist, Sishath Shifaze and asked her if the divorce situation was really that bleak for women. She said, *Oh no. It used to be that way, but things are much, much better now.* I looked at my guidebook again. It was ten years old.

You can also get married in the Maldives. A lot of people do that, too. As a Muslim country, men are allowed up to four wives if they can afford them. Not many can or even want to be bothered with more than one wife. Most men I asked about multiple wives laughed and said that they had enough trouble keeping one woman happy. Another told me that the government required a minimum monthly income of 10,000 rufiyaa (about $835) to qualify financially for a second wife. My Maldivian business colleague, Ibrahim Hareef, told me that he doubted he'd ever reach that threshold and besides he had one good wife and that was enough for him.

On the subject of multiple wives, last year my friend Phoebe Chan, a travel agent at Kota Kinabalu, Malaysia, told me about a Muslim bus driver who had three wives. One wife was a school teacher, another an engineer and the third wife was a social worker. They all made more money than the bus driver and they were smart, too. They worked as a team at home with the teacher taking care of the kids, the engineer volunteering for house cleaning duties, and the social worker stating, I am the youngest, I will take care of the man. Household harmony, who would think it possible under impossible circumstances?

A lot of people go to the Maldives on honeymoons or second honeymoons. That's good when it works well. Sometimes it doesn't. While staying at Thulhagiri Island, amidst young and older couples walking hand-in-hand on pretty white beaches, one of the second honeymooners, a couple from London had a nasty disagreement. For his part, the husband used barnyard language by calling his wife a cow. It hurt her feelings, and she retaliated by getting on the next flight back to the UK. Upon arrival back home, she called, they made up and presumably both learned the value of leaving farm animals out of angry conversations. The story has a happier ending as she returned on the next flight for more romantic strolls on the beach.

There is much to be learned about the world and there are two best ways to do that: reading books and meeting people. Fortunately I find myself in the position of giving thanks daily for the blessings that allow me to do both.

Losing the Mental Challenge

Recently I received an e-mail from Betsy McManus. Betsy is a former neighbor in Virginia and she wrote to thank me for sending some small Christmas gifts to neighborhood kids. As a postscript, she mentioned that she had found two identification cards in the package and wondered if I'd like them returned. They had disappeared at about the time I mailed the package, but never having been too good at math I didn't put 2 and 2 together.

I possess an official passport, tourist passport, retired U.S. Navy ID card, US government ID card, Virginia driver's license, and professional credentials. They all have my picture and are considered to be important. As a long term employee, my agency has higher expectations of me than that I lose things so I am not going to mention Betsy's discovery to anyone at the office. They wouldn't understand how I could mistakenly mail two important ID cards to kids 8,000 miles away. I don't understand either.

If this were an isolated incident I would not think much of it; however, there is a pattern. I started noticing a deterioration of my attention to detail in 1998. That fall I taught a first-time session of 25 adult students who had come together to improve their communication skills in a Speechcraft Workshop sponsored by Toastmasters International. The pair of shoes I wore weren't really a matched set—one was black and one was brown. I didn't realize the error until the class had been concluded for 8-hours. The next day, I called three students to ask if they had noticed anything out of the ordinary. I was comforted when the first two said, *No, I didn't, why do you ask?* With a smile, I replied with a bit of mystery, *Oh, just wondering.* When the third student was asked, she burst into laughter, and then explained that I had worn two different shoes and she thought that was strange. I asked: *Why didn't you tell me?* Her response, *Well, I don't know you very well and I thought you might be an absent-minded professor.* Echoes of the words idiot and moron came to mind.

In 2000, I went to a mailbox in Herndon, Virginia, dropping nine envelopes into the slot; eight of them were stamped and had an address. Inside the unstamped, unaddressed ninth envelop were several checks for $1,800. In the spirit that there are personal events so agonizing you don't share them with anyone, I didn't. After mentally kicking myself as a disciplinary measure, I noted that the mailman would make a collection at the box at 7 am the next morning. Eagerly arriving at the box 15-minutes early, it was disheartening to find that the mailman chose that day to be extra early.

Calling the nice people at the United States Postal Service, I explained the circumstances. They told me that my envelop was being processed along with 15 million other pieces of mail that day at the Dulles Processing and Distribution Center—my hopes of recovering the envelop faded. However, I was assured that they would have my wayward envelop back to me within four days. They kept their word.

A year ago, I lost my Virginia driver's license. Several months later I made application for a new one through an Internet application process. The new card arrived in Singapore at about the time the lost one did. It seems I had given the license to a car dealer in Virginia while selling my car and forgot to reclaim it.

I now keep eyeglasses in every room of my home and have only lost four Singapore metro train passes in the past year. I keep a big supply of umbrellas and have been thinking of chaining my wallet to my trousers. That seems to work well for motorcyclists. I solved the lost car key problem by not having a car. My travel agent tells me my flight schedule, and then he repeats it. I know he is telling me twice, so does he, we both know why he does that. Singapore Airlines, my air carrier of choice, knows that I misplace tickets. They often charge a service fee to correct personal mistakes, but don't do that to me. I don't know why.

When I travel, I leave a trail of forgotten clothes, usually jogging shorts and shirts that I hang out on hotel balconies. None have ever been returned and I don't expect that they will be. Before I forget it, Betsy can you please return my two ID cards!

The Lunar New Year

It's the start of the Lunar New Year. We're experiencing fireworks, face painting, loud drums echoing a beat for the lion and dragon dancers, and there are red lanterns in Chinese communities around the world celebrating the start of a new deal. People are excited. Last year's sheep is out, we're now getting used to the Year of the Monkey.

It's supposed to be a good year, that's what the Singaporean taxi drivers tell me and they aren't a particularly optimistic crowd. All this monkey business started about 5,000 years ago when the Great Buddha summoned all the animals together for a party. For whatever reasons, only 12 showed up. With gratitude for this effort, Buddha promised them that he would honor each with their own year. That's how Year of the Monkey got its start along with years for the horse, dragon, sheep, rabbit, rat, snake, pig, dog, cow, tiger, and chicken.

My daughters Christina and Mary are monkeys, I am a horse, and my manicurist, Lai Li Lian, is a dragon—I think these are good signs. Even though all of them are the original party animals, I'd rather not be a rat, snake, pig, or chicken. Over the years one person or another has called me all those names, sometimes unfairly; even when I might have deserved it, I didn't like the comments. Part of being a well-adjusted adult is accepting reality with grace. Be that as it may, it's a shame that Buddha could not have made a concession for the elephants so that some of us could be born in the Year of the Elephant. I suppose it's too late for adjustments.

Chinese people around the world use the holiday to sweep away the past to open up the future for good luck and that's not a bad idea. *Out with the old and in with the new*, as we say during the other New Year's holiday.

Red is the Chinese lucky color and foods and customs revolve around the themes of happiness, wealth and longevity. They like to eat fish for togetherness and abundance; noodles for long life; and chickens with the head, tail and feet for completeness. I don't eat all these foods which may explain why my past and future sometimes seem just so-so.

One of the other interesting foods favored by the Chinese is jiaozi, dumplings boiled in water. This symbolism means sleep well together and you will have sons; however, eating jiaozi comes with no guarantees. You may sleep well together and have daughters. That will happen half the time and it's a good thing. Cherry blossoms, peach blossoms, sweet olive plumes, and cattails are all ornate features in stores and homes. Families use the first several weeks of the New Year to travel back to their homelands, visit relatives and spend time with neighbors. The adults love playing cards and board games, and the kids, just like kids everywhere, enjoy reunions with their cousins.

Following church services a year ago at the Lunar New Year, I noticed parishioners passing red packets to the children. A gray-haired Australian man told me that the red packets contained money and were given to children and single people. Honoring children and single people with money seems like a nice touch especially for the recipient.

Nearly 77 percent of Singapore's population is of Chinese origin. That amounts to about 3.5 million people. The remainder traces their ancestry mostly to India and Malaysia. Like people everywhere, the Chinese love their families.

That's why Lee Lin En and his wife Soon Yue Chan are having a tough time right now. On December 21, their daughter Sharon, 34, collapsed at a family gathering. A vessel in her brain had burst; four days later she was brain dead. There aren't any silver linings in tragic losses of this nature; however, Madam Soon did insure that Sharon's organs were donated to give new life to at least three people—a 54-year old woman and a 42-year old man received her kidneys, and a 17-month old girl received her liver. For three people it's more than the start of the Lunar New Year, its rebirth. The Lee family members had all pledged their organs in 1982. Their decision wasn't based on being born under one animal sign or another, or that they had been eating certain foods. They did it because of extraordinary compassion and love, two qualities that are always in style. More important than all the ceremony involved in moving us from one lunar year to the next, the Lee family has given us all the gift of their example.

The world needs an extraordinary good year. Our Year of the Monkey may be that great year if we think happiness and completeness, sleep well together, honor children, and show love and compassion.

Snakes

For the past few days I've been thinking about snakes. Most people don't like snakes. I understand that because I don't either. The few people who really like snakes become herpetologists or just seem odd to the rest of us. Herpetologists do their best to get us to like snakes. They mostly fail although they work hard at studying them, doing research, and then telling us what remarkable creatures they are.

Everybody has fears that they grow up with. Mine were bears and snakes. As a little kid, they were in my bad dreams. Gradually I came to not mind bears so much and now enjoy seeing pandas and polar bears from a distance. They're especially appealing when playing with their zoo toys or rolling around with one another in innocent fun.

Years ago, I served on a US Navy ship in the South China Sea. We sailed the coastal waters of Vietnam, Cambodia, and Thailand. Everyday I'd go up on deck and take in the watery scene around me. On good days, the limitless royal blue sky blended in perfect harmonious color with still waters and occasionally I'd see sea snakes passing on their journey to somewhere. Sometimes there were hundreds. Oddly, they were always going in the opposite direction of the ship.

Our captain was an enterprising leader who had concerns about boredom with the officers and crew. He encouraged all the officers to accept an identity associated with a fox. The captain was the gray fox, the supply officer was the cheap fox, and the executive officer was the sly fox. They all had their fox names embroidered on dark blue baseball caps. Sometimes he'd stop the ship, we'd throw a cargo net over the side and life rings into the water and sailors would jump over the side for a swim. I never did that.

There have never been more snakes, at least it seems that way because of the Discovery Channel, Animal Planet, and National Geographic Society television programming. What we are fortunate enough to miss in nature comes to us in terrifying detail in the comfort of our own homes. I don't watch these programs and have little empathy for those that do. When deciding whether I should relocate to Singapore. I had two concerns: Will it be too hot to jog and will I see snakes?

Jogging near the equator isn't too bad for 5-10 miles, after that heat takes a toll. Singapore has snakes, apparently a lot of them, many are poisonous—the paradise tree snake, one of the more deadly ones, climbs trees and jumps in the direction of its targeted victim. They don't do this for recreation; there is always a targeted victim. They have learned to flatten their bodies out to skillfully glide and undulate to this target. Fortunately it doesn't prey on humans. In my first few months of jogging in early morning darkness, I saw six snakes: Two road kills, one sleeping on a sidewalk grate, two water snakes swimming in a canal, and in a rain forest there was a bright blue snake with an orange-red neon stripe along each side. It was a banded Malayan coral snake, poisonous, but not the least bit interested in me.

In the summer of 2002, I understand that in broad daylight a large boa constrictor crossed five lanes of busy traffic on Orchard Road in Singapore. It was migrating from the Thai Embassy to a trash container across the street. Heavy traffic stopped, pedestrians stared in awe. After it crawled into its new home in the trash container, snake people from pest control arrived to transport the snake to another home somewhere less threatening to us humans. I have a Singaporean friend who works in pest control. He confirms that snakes can be a nuisance, but that wasps and bees are worse.

A few days ago, I came to work to learn that a snake was loose in the office. Depending on whom I spoke with it varied in length from a few inches to a few feet. Those who hadn't seen it tended toward the larger size. Our supervisor did the right thing; he got a small flashlight and started looking underneath furniture. With equal enthusiasm, I went on a coffee break. Julie Seckel, new to the office, followed. With anxiety in her voice, she explained that she hated snakes. I nodded in understanding.

On returning from the break, my workmates had cornered the snake beneath a shredder. Without realizing my past relationship with serpents, someone suggested that I watch that spot and if the snake attempted to escape I should stomp on it. I listened to the instructions, looked at the shredder, and thought of my Buddhist friends who feel guilty if they squash a mosquito.

Within minutes the snake people arrived to give our guest a new home. It was probably about 10 inches long, just a baby. Initially the snake man thought it to be a reticulated python; however, a more thorough check revealed that it was a rare Malaysian racer and nonpoisonous. Although I've been thinking of snakes, there haven't been any nightmares. Perhaps it is true that we do improve with age.

Hungry Ghosts and Ancestry

Imagine that you've been having a tough time for the past year; in fact, it's been so bad you haven't eaten in all that time and you're a little grouchy. I know you're thinking that if you didn't eat for a year you'd be dead, and that's the point.

It is the seventh month of the lunar calendar and if you're Chinese you know that means there are now hungry ghosts in our midst. For the rest of us, it is a time to watch and wonder. The Hungry Ghost festival has its genesis in Buddhism and Chinese religious traditions that promote honoring one's ancestors.

It all started 1,500 years ago and now encompasses a full month. The ghosts bring good fortune to those on earth if they are treated well on their annual visit. Treating ghosts well has come to mean nighttime bonfires in which paper houses, cars, clothes, money and other valuables are burned as an offering to the wandering spirits. During the day, the air is filled with burning incense and gifts of food and drink are offered at improvised shrines.

Everyone wants the ghosts to have a happy time during their breath of fresh air. Some of these spirits are probably from their permanent homes very deep in the earth, if you are not good at taking hints, that's Hell. Not all of them are well-behaved ghosts nor were they perfect in life. Chinese parents explain to their youngsters about the need to be wary because some ancestors, not necessarily their own may be given to spooky tricks. To be safe from peril, there are safety precautions: don't walk in the ashes of the sacrificial bonfires, don't stay out late, travel or swim (especially in the ocean); and it's definitely not the right time to marry. It is okay strolling hand-in-hand, hugging, kissing, and whispering sweet nothings, just don't get married.

The Chinese are renowned for their smart business sense so let's make an assumption they aren't burning real money, it is more of a symbolic gesture. My ancestors were not that good at business and wouldn't understand if I didn't burn real money. They'd think, *Hey, we're worth the real thing, you cheapskate*. Then when the Hungry Ghost festival was over, they'd stay on to haunt me. It doesn't seem fair, but that's the way some families are. All that said, I guess there's nothing for me to be sorry about, I am not Chinese and my ancestors aren't out roaming the earth. Even at that I am watching, wondering and hoping a hungry ghost may generously donate good fortune at my door step. I've been going to bed early!

Wandering the earth and honoring relatives is something we humans do well. Tomorrow Virasak Phonphibsvads leaves Paris with his daughter Kham to visit their fatherland, Laos. This is a dad and daughter pilgrimage. In 1979, Virasak moved his family from Laos to France in search of a safe, secure and more prosperous future. The family was part of an exodus of 30,000 people who entered France from Laos to escape political turmoil.

Kham was only 2-years old and although she now speaks four languages, possesses a university degree and has traveled extensively, she had never returned to her homeland and doesn't know her grandfather, that's Virasak's dad. He's over 80 years old. Introductions will be taken care of as father and daughter travel back in time through the Laotian cities of Vientiane and Pakse. At the end of their trip they will better understand roots and their relationship with each other, it is inevitable. Using our past as a touchstone for the future brings good fortune.

Fifteen years ago, I visited western Indiana to see where some of my ancestors had lived. In 1818, they were early pioneers in the wilderness near Lafayette, traded with Indians, and cleared the land for farming. And their ancestors were patriots in America's Revolutionary War. Standing on the fields where they stood and seeing the old farmhouse where my grandmother and mother were born transformed me to pride in ancestry. I visited the Pretty Prairie Cemetery, saw ancestral gravestones, and felt a good spirit. I walked across the land seeing some of what they had seen, there were rocks they moved and trees they had planted. My ancestors didn't have an easy life, yours probably didn't either. They worked exceedingly hard to not just survive but over several generations they had genuinely prospered. I also realized that their qualities of faith, hope, and optimism where my qualities, all I had to do was use them.

Traveling back in time to learn more about ancestry changes people whether it's learning about hungry ghosts, a dad and his daughter connecting to roots, or a pilgrim like me feeling a spiritual heritage. When we look back and reflect on what our legacy means there is an enlightenment that naturally flows our way. Now that's good fortune.

The Right Place for Good Fortune

Good fortune falls to those who are in the right place at the right time. Just as likely we unwittingly become trapped by bad fortune when caught in the wrong place. That latter thought was the spiritual theme of Rabbi Harold Kushner's book, *When Bad Things Happen to Good People.*

Two weeks ago, I was on travel through Ho Chi Minh City, Hanoi and Haiphong, an experience that left me with good memories and a better appreciation for the world's nooks and crannies where so much of life is taking place.

Ho Chi Minh City, with 10 million people, is in southern Vietnam and oriented toward the USA; Hanoi and Haiphong (5.1 million in combined population) are cities in the north and there you find more French speakers and the wonders of French colonial architecture. Hanoi was once the capital of French Indochina (Laos, Cambodia and Vietnam). Past hostilities notwithstanding, the Vietnamese are warm and friendly toward Americans and those met on the street enjoyed practicing whatever English they knew. Two years ago, the Pew Charitable Trust in Washington, DC, did a worldwide survey of global attitudes. Sixty-eight percent of the Vietnamese polled liked America's ideas about democracy. It is currently a communist country.

As in all Vietnamese cities, life is publicly abundant on the streets from early morning until after sunset. The Vietnamese are up earlier and more active than people in other Asian countries. By 5 am, the parks are busy with enthused badminton and volleyball players, and groups practicing slow-motion tai chi; the streets are starting to fill with bicycles and motorbikes; curbside restaurants are preparing breakfast meals of noodles, rice porridge, boiled spinach, and bread; a few kids are rollerblading, and venders are rubbing the sleep from their eyes for another day. By 7:30 am, the nets are down, most people gone, and the park benches occupied by old men and women talking as they wait for something to happen in the passing scene.

While in Hanoi, I jogged around Hoan Kiem Lake in the early mornings. On one of those mornings I saw nearly a hundred people staring out into the lake. If you've never noticed, there's nothing more tempting than to stop whatever you're doing and stare off into space when given a human example to follow. It's akin to seeing a person open their mouth wide in a satisfying yawn. Before you know it, you can't help yourself from doing it, too.

In following the crowd's gaze across the lake I saw a football shaped head moving through the water. Behind what turned out to be a huge head was a broad trailing wake. It's hard to judge the size of this old mariner, but a specimen taken from the lake several years earlier was nearly 7 feet long and weighed over 500 pounds. Because these turtle sightings are so rare the Vietnamese believe that anyone fortunate enough to see one is bound for good luck and that's what I am planning.

It's great when you're in the right place for good fortune. My other outstanding recollection from Hoan Kiem Lake is the old ladies lined up in ranks slowly moving bright silver swords to the rhythm of semi-classical music. It was my first time, outside of the movies, to see women with swords. Some of the other women's groups exercising around the lake used flags as part of their routine; others tossed basketballs. To witness the purposeful concentration and state of satisfaction on the wrinkled and creased faces of the elderly is to see human beauty at its best.

Haiphong has a workforce of 936,000 people, 40,000 are university or college graduates. The economy is based on the export of rice and timber, shipbuilding, fishing, tourism, agriculture and light manufacturing. Haiphong maintains a sister city relationship with Seattle, Washington, which primarily involves Seattle-based community service organizations providing much needed aid for the disadvantaged, particularly children.

Vietnam has about 20,000 homeless kids, 1,600 are in Hanoi. Some are cared for, others are exploited. Many of them, 12-18 years old, attempt fending for themselves by selling small books, maps, postcards and chewing gum to tourists. Their prices are inflated; my workmates and I empty our pockets. After so many needless purchases, we simply make donations. The per capita income in Vietnam is $2,300 annually. The street kids earn about $3 a month to defray costs of housing and school. One evening I saw two young men strong arm a girl in extorting her postcard earnings. She was in tears and in frustration muttered, *why did I have to be born in Vietnam*? I also wonder about the meaning of where and when we're born.

Poultry farmers are suffering horribly in Vietnam. To date, they've destroyed over 36 million chickens because of the Asian bird flu, 15 people have died, and KFC in Saigon has converted to fish. The World Bank, headquartered in Washington, DC, has put up $10 million in loans to help Vietnam's poultry industry recover. The World Bank does good work in developing countries. It has been working with the British government to support a road improvement program in Vietnam that will eventually cost $200 million to upgrade surfaces along 8,000 miles of rural roadway.

In one little country, in one short week, I saw daily examples of people happy with their circumstances, others weren't as satisfied. Being in the right place at the right time makes a difference; however, in fairness maybe somebody should write a book, *When Good Things Happen to Good People.*

Mount Kinabalu

The past few weeks have given me uncountable happy, peaceful moments in Bali, Malaysia, and Thailand. While I was living my great life other people in the world were having their own ups and downs. My coworker in Singapore, John Smallman, was on a definite high in climbing Mount Fuji in Japan. Like all men, John expresses himself in manspeak. In passionately explaining the meaning for his climb, he told me *...it was a real asskicker.* Because I had climbed Mount Kinabalu in Malaysia at about the same time, I thought his remark reasonable.

Mr. Ong Hock Siew of Singapore probably has a different view. This chap has climbed Mount Kinabalu on 47 occasions. He leads youth and church groups on the climb. When I mentioned to John that Mr. Ong probably finds the experience cleansing for his soul, John mused that one trip up the mountain was enough scrubbing for his lifetime.

In trekking up Mount Kinabalu, I associated with positive, energetic people, some fit for the experience, others not. My guide was Victor Siam, his great-grandfather, Gulyting bin Lagadan, was the first licensed guide for Mount Kinabalu. Certainly the mountain is haunted, everyone says that it is. The Dusun, a tribe of indigenous people live nearby, their ancestors were headhunters and made human sacrifices on the mountain's slopes. It helps in the promotion of eco-tourism that these days they forego the human experience and now use white chickens in their sacrificial ceremonies.

Lifetime education is incomplete without the exhilaration of climbing a mountain. The exquisite beauty and the exercise of sheer willpower to move beyond normal endurance redefine the inner spirit making us better in the process.

The Japanese certainly believe this is true as people of all ages move up their national mountain, Mount Fujiyama, looking upon it as a once in a lifetime experience. Mount Kinabalu is more isolated and perhaps more difficult. The trail is restricted to just 170 climbers a day with everyone required to have a guide. I am glad I had Victor. As a second year university student in botany, he was a fountain of knowledge on plant life along the steep trail.

Most of the climb is through a rainforest canopy that shades the trail from the sun and provides shelter from monsoon rains. It rained heavily during my climb. The ground was carpeted with bright green moss and algae, small flowers and tiny wild orchids naturally rooted in tree trunks and on limbs, a few birds flitted about and butterflies fluttered at lower elevations, we passed waterfalls and heard the rush of running water in the distance. At higher elevations trees grow progressively smaller, lichen covers the trees, and ultimately there is nothing but solid rock, wind, and sky. It feels like the top of the world. Through most of the climb there was a pleasant stillness, the silence disturbed only by the rush of water, a frog, cricket and occasionally a distant human voice. The rain fell, souls were cleansed, oxygen thinned, I tired easily and rested, but never lost my sense of joy at climbing the mountain.

There were a few covered rest stops, outdoor toilets, and tanks filed with refreshing mountain water. I met three Frenchmen; ironically I was wearing a polo shirt with the French flag prominently displayed on the front.

I introduced myself, they smiled, and their English was excellent. The devil made me say, with a straight face, that I'd given up eating French fries until I either lost ten pounds or they got their country squared away. They roared, we agreed that whatever differences Presidents Bush and Chirac have, we were going to enjoy our time together climbing the mountain. Younger, stronger and better conditioned, they were soon far ahead, my thought on giving up French fries returned. The temperature cooled with the increase in elevation, the Japanese passed me, and then came the Italians, a few people were coming down from their climb a day earlier. One lady was being carried; several others looked like they needed to be carried. Soon I'd be heading down. When that happened I was disappointed to learn that going down was just as hard as going up.

Climbing the mountain gave me a chance to be part of a different world, see small things, and feel my own insignificance. John was right in his assessment that the exertion was humbling and I understand why Mr. Ong would climb Mount Kinabalu again and again. The experience was a component in what comprises living a good life, moving forward a step at a time, sometimes an inch at a time, not giving up, maintaining a good spirit...re-igniting the inner flame and setting a good example when the going gets tough. I'd do it again and the truth is John probably would, too!

Exotic India

Several weeks ago, I got wet in Mumbai, India. August is a monsoon month and it rained for the six days and nights that I was there. I thought about the ark and even related the story of Noah's heroic effort to several cab drivers.

Mumbai has a spirit of sound and sight that is little affected by rain, even if it lasts nearly a week. The streets are alive with women in colorful saris and gold jewelry; men dressed in dhotis, a loose white garment pulled up between the legs; and children in their neatly pressed school uniforms. Most are either talking on their cell phones or have one in their pocket.

Streets are noisy from the incessant honking of anxious taxi drivers and the air is filled with the mixed smells of sidewalk food venders, aromatic herbs, and diesel exhaust from aged, red doubled-deck buses. There are beggars, con artists, pickpockets, and tourists from Germany, France, and Japan. The merchants aren't as honest as they should be and there is energy everywhere you look except with the cows. Even though they are sacred, they still looked a little sad living on the street. There was no pasture in sight and they plopped wherever they happened to be standing.

Buildings are picturesque Victorians in need of repair. They were built by the British during colonial times and there doesn't seem to have been much construction since.

Sidewalk snake charmers are gone with their flutes and cobras. That's a good thing. Their days became numbered in 1972 when India passed a law protecting wildlife.

Sixteen million people live in Mumbai, which was called Bombay until 1998. The world is changing and it's more than names. There are 60,000 Americans living in India while 3.2 million Indian-Americans live in the USA. Thirty-eight percent of American doctors are Indians. Indians in America are slightly better educated, make slightly more money, and have slightly larger families that native born Americans. Some of the jobs that used to be done in America, Australia, and Great Britain have shifted to India. That makes them happy and frustrates the losers.

There are world famous people associated with India that we look up to with fond remembrance: Mahatma Gandhi inspired the world to seek social change through nonviolent civil disobedience; Indira Gandhi was an early role model for women in statesmanship; and Mother Teresa taught the world the meaning of compassion.

Some of us are famous in India. In 2002, Bill Gates donated 100 million dollars to benefit HIV/AIDS research and treatment. They like him a lot. Another popular American is Richard Gere who supports HIV/AIDS clinics through the Gere Foundation. Eight months ago, he visited the Red Light District in the Kamathipura neighborhood. There are 10,000 prostitutes crowded into a small area and his public time with a few of them further emphasized the importance of HIV/AIDS prevention and treatment. For about half of them it's too late to prevent infection.

I also found several dozen people who remembered The Reverend George Bowen. He was the American missionary who 115 years ago founded what would become the Bowen Memorial Church. I attended the English service there along with 22 Indians. Before the service I probably overemphasized to the minister that I was a Presbyterian, but that Methodists were among my favorite friends. He laughed at the time and later introduced me to the congregation using those terms. That earned me a weak smile from the people seated nearby.

While in Mumbai, I met Jodie, Rati, and Roger---three beggar children. They were 12, 9, and 7, respectively. There are thousands of beggars in Mumbai, a reported thousand or so are organized under the King of Beggars, an entrepreneur who came to Mumbai seeking opportunity 15 years ago. He found his niche by organizing the beggars and then taking a cut of the action. Many of the professional beggars are more affluent that people in other industries. They own nice cars and homes and are resented by their neighbors. Children and women with a baby in their arms are artful in describing the horrors of their life of hunger and deprivation. It all sounds so sad one can scarcely resist parting with a few rupees on the chance that the stories might be true. Jodie, Rati, and Roger don't like being called beggars so they give flower bracelets made from fragrant jasmine. The kids help visitors by explaining local customs and where to find the best shopping areas. The value they add is by acting as peanut gallery tour guides. At an appropriate time they politely ask for a donation.

During my stay, the Mumbai community suffered a tragedy. One of the people they looked up to committed suicide. Nafisa Joseph was 25 years old and a former Miss India. Since then she had become a successful actress, model and VJ on MTV. After a row with her fiancé, she became deeply depressed and hung herself. If there is a lesson that Nafisa's sad end can teach us it's to never lose heart.

Besides the monsoon rains that bring street flooding, Mumbai is a sea of human chaos. From my view of travel I see three good parts. The departure, the return and what goes on in between. In visiting Mumbai, the best part was getting back to Singapore's order and discipline, and of course, the blue skies and sunshine. Sometimes we don't know how good we have it.

Amy and Denise

The quality of our lives is dependent on the quality of our relationships. When you possess compassion, respect and understanding – those kinds of attributes are mirrored back making your life more purposeful and rewarding. I am reminded of this premise in the story of Amy Cruz and Denise O' Brien.

In 2001, both were 30ish age women employed by the Visa Corporation – Amy in San Francisco while Denise worked in McLean, a Virginia suburb of Washington, DC. They met at a conference earlier that year. Several months later Denise learned that Amy had been diagnosed with breast cancer. When a woman receives a life-threatening diagnosis of breast cancer, she thinks of many things. In Amy's case, she thought of her two small children, her husband, and how much she still wanted to live. She was frightened as any normal person would be.

Sensing the situation by long-distance, Denise reached out to Amy through telephone calls and e-mails. Denise wanted to do something that would inspire Amy. Discussing the situation with co-workers, the Visa office in McLean came up with an idea. They would enter a running and walking team dedicated to Amy in Washington's National Race for the Cure. After registering the team, *Cruzin' for a Cure*, they learned about fund raising – held car washes and sold donuts to people in their building. The team raised $6,000 to benefit breast cancer research and treatment through The Susan G. Komen Breast Cancer Foundation.

In the meantime, Amy proceeded with radiation and chemotherapy. Her cancer went into remission, the future brightened and she was able to walk with *Cruzin' for a Cure* in Washington. As you might suspect, this experience was vitally important to Amy as was the compassionate relationship between the two women.

In 2002, Amy's cancer metastasized (spread) becoming active in other parts of her body eventually affecting her collarbone, hips, back and finally the liver. As she received the best treatments medical science could provide, *Cruzin' for a Cure* continued fund raising, and Denise kept up her long-distance encouragement. The team, fellow employees and their families prayed for Amy as she fought a difficult battle for her life.

In her final week, Denise visited Amy in a California hospital. She told her she loved her, a final gift between the spiritual sisters. Amy died August 22, 2004. Husband Mike and children Jenice and Brandon survive her. Over the past few years I've often thought of these two women, once strangers, who came together at the right time to change both of their lives for the better. The details of it inspire me and I hope that in its retelling at this time of Amy's passing it will mean something to a relationship you may have that requires an extra measure of compassion and kindness.

Vasco da Gama Was Right

In 1492, Christopher Columbus left Cadiz, Spain, sailing in search of a sea passage to India, China, and Indonesia. In October of that year, he discovered the Caribbean and for the remainder of his life he never gave up on the idea that Haiti was Japan, Cuba was China, and South America was some sort of biblical paradise. America celebrates Christopher with an annual holiday, this year it is October 11.

Vasco da Gama set out from Portugal in 1497 in search of India, China, and Indonesia. On Christmas Day of that year he landed at Calicut, a spot on the southwest coast of India. There aren't many celebrations for Vasco except at Goa, India. They love him.

Last week I was at Goa, a Portuguese colony from 1498 until 1961. It is now one of the 28 states that comprise India. The people there aren't happy about being called Indians, their pride lies in being referred to as Portuguese descendants and Goans.

Goa is a geographical gem. The people live well there, but as a friend, Captain Bruno D'Souza, told me: *We're not rich, but everyone has enough.* Goa has the highest per capital income in India and at 76 percent, one of the highest literacy rates. The area is rural with an abundance of cows, chickens, pigs, dogs, goats, and kids wandering around farmsteads that dot the countryside of verdant rice paddies, swaying palm trees, and miles of pretty beaches. Cows like to sleep on the narrow country roads at night, driving isn't safe, but tourists don't seem to care and local residents accept it as a way-of-life. The vacationers come from Russia, Japan, Canada, Australia, Germany, Spain and other European countries to live on the beaches, swim in clean water, and eat slightly spicy Goan seafood. Like me, they see small herds of cows ambling down the middle of a highway, traffic stops, sometimes there are herders, sometimes not – no one seems to mind. Patience is plentiful, that's part of the appeal.

Goa is a small Indian state with just 1.4 million people. Besides beaches, the major attraction is Old Goa, a fascinating little town known for its churches. The oldest, Chapel of St. Catherine, was built in 1510 and the most prominent is Se Cathedral, which is the largest church in Asia. Standing beside Se Cathedral is Basilica of Born Jesus where the remains of St. Francis Xavier are entombed. Francis Xavier was the most significant missionary of his time and a founder of the Jesuits. Thirty percent of Goans are Christians; the remainder is Hindu with a small group of Muslims.

Seafaring visitors at the town of Vasco da Gama, a small seaport on the coast, used to stop by the area's red light district. A few months ago that tourist attraction was razed. As the buildings were destroyed, 1,506 people who specialize in petty crime, drugs, and sex were expelled from Goa. Who says the world isn't getting better?

Since leaving Goa my jogging shoes have been squeaking from being wet. It's the monsoon season in Southern India – during my time there it mostly rained, but don't get the impression that that isn't good. As I discovered, one of life's great pleasures is jogging along country roads under a canopy of overarching palm trees as the charcoal skies drizzle. The sights are memorable: the peep squeak brigade and school teachers riding their bikes to nearby schools, a few dogs giving barking threats (I tell them soothingly what good dogs they are thinking God will forgive a small fib now and then), and there is the clickety-clack of an antiquated passenger train not far off.

Last March in Goa, one of my workmates was bitten by one of these neighborhood dogs. He said the resulting rabies vaccination was of some discomfort. As I jog, kids grin and stare, it's the gaze of children seeing something for the first time – you can almost see their mental wheels whirling as they puzzle through a new sight, someone running for the joy of running. They don't know what to make of it and that makes me smile with my own wonder at the innocence we're sometimes fortunate enough to find. Kids aren't the only ones who find strangers interesting to look at. Cows are also curious and tend to stare, as do old people sitting on their front porches. I waved at the people and stared back at the cows. All the humans were friendly – they nodded, smiled and sometimes said hello; and the cows – they seem to like the eye contact.

Christopher Columbus was wrong about his geography and that pleases Americans, Vasco da Gama was right and the Goans couldn't be more satisfied. Japan is where it should be, Cuba isn't China, and the cows roam freely at Goa. It can be a confusing world at times, but most things turn out okay in spite of our occasional misjudgments.

Selamat Datang

Selamat datang is a phrase you often hear in Indonesia. It means welcome! Last week I was on business travel there and I couldn't have been more thrilled. Although most people aren't jumping out of their skin to visit Indonesia, I was happy to be there. I wanted to experience firsthand the diversity of an environment that produces international headlines. For several hundred years it was called the East Indies, a colony exploited for its mineral wealth and spices. When the Dutch departed in 1950, the capital of Batavia became Jakarta and Indonesia was born as a nation.

Indonesia is an important relative in the world family – just consider that it is the fourth largest country (after China, India, and USA) with 238 million people, has more Muslims than any other nation, and has some of the richest natural resources (gold, silver, oil and natural gas, nickel, and such). However, all that glitters is not gold. The country has a reputation for being one of the most corrupt nations in the world, and pirates prey on shipping that passes near its shores. Indonesians speak 300 different languages – Bahasa Indonesian (a pure form of Malay) is the first official language with English a distant second.

There are Buddhists, Hindus, Arabs, Chinese, Malays and Europeans living on 19,000 islands that have a hundred active volcanoes. If you visit and feel the ground shaking it is from one of the frequent earthquakes, fortunately most of these are small tremors. The main islands are Sumatra, Java, and Bali, where if you're on an unlucky stroll through the rainforest you could chance upon a tiger, crocodile, or a poisonous snake – the luckier among us would see elephants, monkeys or richly colored birds.

If there is one thing more deadly than poisonous snakes it is terrorists. In the past few years there have been major terrorist bomb attacks in Jakarta and Bali that were directed against Westerners (Americans and Australians). Besides that, churches in Jakarta have been bombed by people who carry a grudge against Christians. Indonesians are warmly affectionate toward Westerners, well not everyone is, but 99.9 percent greet you with a smile and mean it. However, like most countries there is a lunatic fringe that bears watching.

Indonesians are among the friendliest and most positive souls in Asia. While I was in Jakarta the World Bank released its annual report on bribery and business. Indonesia isn't the worst offender in the world. Those ahead of it are China, Cambodia, and Russia.

After three long days in Jakarta, I flew 400 miles east to Surabaya to a happier time. Surabaya is cleaner and the human touch more intimate with just three million people. It was in Surabaya that I got lost while jogging. As bad luck would have it I left the hotel filled with energy and a fun spirit. Unfortunately, about once a year I find myself directionally challenged.

In 2003, I got lost in Singapore and was so late for work that I had to call in sick with embarrassment. This time I was jogging on narrow, curvy streets through an outdoor market, down a hill, around a bend and before I knew it I had lost east and west as well as north and south. Uncertainty filled the void. I was reminded of the importance of understanding the left from the right as I tried to learn from passersby the best route back to my hotel.

Everyone knew, but in converting the information from Bahasa to English several people did what I did when I was learning words as a little boy. I confused right and left. After three people sent me further away than closer I realized we weren't communicating with the specificity needed; however, there is no substitute for persistence when it comes to following bewildering directions and all's well that eventually ends well. I found the hotel.

Surabaya is also home to Plaza Tunjungan, the largest shopping mall in Indonesia. It has 500 stores, restaurants, cinemas, nightclubs, and an ice skating rink. Included in the mall are familiar names like Starbucks, McDonalds, KFC, Pizza Hut, and Fizziwig's Candy Factory. The Sheraton Hotel is an anchor of the complex where people shop for American, European, and Asian jewelry, clothing, perfumes, toys, music, and children's wear. It is upscale. Surabaya is famous for its Dutch architecture, ornate temples and mosques, and international cuisine. Outside of town the countryside contains lush coffee and tea plantations and beautiful fruit orchards.

After getting bumped off my flight with Indonesian's flag carrier, Garuda Airlines, I spent another day in Surabaya before flying 200 miles east to Denpasar, Bali. This is the Bali of beautiful white beaches, gently swaying palms, and blue waters. Interestingly, the people there are 98 percent Hindu and the number of area temples reflects a populace devoted to their religion. Besides the belt-busting great food, I had several memorable runs near Kuta Beach.

One morning near the end of a run, I met Dyu. She was riding a motorcycle and stopped to ask if I needed a lift. I didn't, but being a street smart bachelor, I accepted one anyway. Before getting on, I asked Dyu if she was a good driver. She laughed and vigorously shook her head no. As I wondered whether she was kidding, we were off into a traffic-weaving pattern. The fragrance of her pretty black hair blowing in the breeze said she was using a shampoo with traces of frangipani, an Asian tree often grown near temples and pagodas for the sweet scene of its blossoms. Arriving at the hotel entrance, we came to a screeching halt and a hundred tourists looked up at the improbable sight of a gray-haired white guy riding behind a lovely brown-skinned woman driving a motorcycle. I alighted with a grin. She smiled. After thanking her, I asked, *do you know your right from the left.* She laughed and said, *sometimes.*

Four interesting events occurred while I was in Indonesia: The first direct presidential election was successfully concluded with former general Susilo Bambang Yudhoyono selected by the people for a five year term. So strong is the spirit of democracy that about 80 percent of the populace turned out to vote. And then there was the noodle scandal in which a number of refugees suffered diarrhea and vomiting after eating expired instant noodles that had unfortunately been distributed by the government. The official responsible couldn't be reached for comment – now isn't that always the way!

And 1,500 dismissed Kasogi workers were protesting to demand severance pay that had been awarded them by a court. Kasogi is a shoe firm that is broke and can't pay. If this sounds American, I'll leave commentary to your imagination.

The last event is inspiring: While jogging at Bali early on October 5, I noted that students from one of the middle schools that wore bright neon blue shorts and white shirts as the day's school uniform were jogging on many side streets. At 6:15 am, I found out why as more boys and girls excitedly tumbled out of the school on their weekly jog. Seeing a teacher in athletic attire, I stopped to learn more and couldn't quite believe it when she said that the students would continue running until 8 am. Because I couldn't believe it, I confirmed the information with a service manager at my hotel. The kids were trim, fit, and eager. Although they are materially poor by Western standards I thought how lucky they were to have this head start on good health.

Selamat means, *May your time be blessed,* and that is the way Indonesians say goodbye.

Family Visit to Singapore

I love Singapore and enjoy showing visitors the local wonders. Most capital cities are interesting places because they fuse culture and custom from a diversity of people who are tapped into global networking.

It's exciting to live in a place where little ideas grow through nurturing by smart people who work hard. Singaporeans could have invented the concept of internationalism, a view that looks beyond the horizon of national boundaries. Resources of this little country (26 miles by 14 miles) are limited to about 4 million people.

The only real natural resource is scenic beauty and that is in abundance. There are large interesting trees, some like the frangipani are loaded with fragrant blossoms that make a person want to breathe more deeply; and colorful shrubs and flowers entertain small birds, butterflies and bees.

Over the past 40 years Singapore has developed itself into one of the most dynamic commercial centers in the world on the strength of innovation. Singaporeans are thinkers who have figured out how they can best get along and prosper in the world community. The fruits of these efforts show in high educational levels, environmental cleanliness, an extremely low crime rate, personal prosperity, home ownership, modern medicine, social welfare, and community pride. Singapore is a center for finance, transportation, light manufacturing, and tourism. They don't sell chewing gum or like jaywalking, spitting, littering, or offending the modesty of a female. And it is the only Asian capital city that does not suffer from air pollution and road congestion. Singapore has one of the world's busiest seaport with 140,000 ship visits annually and Changi International Airport has 24 million people pass through every year (about 8 million stay long enough to be classified as a tourist).

I was reminded of all this a few weeks ago during a family visit. The kin stayed two weeks and included my sister, Linda Freshour; niece Lea Ann Nichols; grandnephew David Nichols, 11; and grandnieces Ashley Nichols, 9, and Erin Nichols, 5-6. The city, island and country of Singapore made it easy for us to enjoy a Christmas spirit, yuletide décor and seasonal music that started appearing about October 23. By the time they arrived on November 12, many of the local residents were in a better mood than usual because of the festive atmosphere. Traveling from Michigan, my family made a big sacrifice in visiting Singapore: kids missed school, but did their homework; expensive airline tickets were purchased; jobs put on hold (we should all do that more); and there was the trauma of traveling 22 hours across 11 time zones via Chicago and Hong Kong.

All of our days together were the best as we laughed through running, swimming, trekking, eating, shopping, riding the metro train, watching dragon boat races and visiting Singapore's botanical garden, zoo, butterfly park, tropical bird park, Chinese mythological park, a Hindu temple, old-fashioned Malay village, Underwater World, the Asian Civilization Museum, and traveling on a day trip to Malaysia. My sister experienced her first trishaw ride and facial massage; Lea Ann opted for her first body massage. For the first time the kids petted a dolphin, rode an elephant, cuddled a banana snake, ate dragon fruit, and swam in the ocean—this one the South China; and Ashley had her first communion.

They shopped on Orchard Road (Singapore's equivalent of New York City's Fifth Avenue), meandered through Chinatown, visited Little India, cruised the Singapore River, and hiked through a rainforest (45 percent of Singapore is rainforest) looking for monkeys and snakes. We were rewarded with the sighting of one monkey, a turtle, monitor lizard, and a rooster that crowed, but didn't see any snakes.

65

Everyone timidly sampled Asian food, but most stuck with their familiar standbys: KFC, Pizza Hut, McDonalds and Burger King.

Singapore's monsoon season starts in November and continues through February. Every day of their visit it rained for several hours. When it wasn't raining, it was warmish and humid. That happens when you are just 85 miles from the Equator.

We had a pool party celebrating Erin's 6th birthday. She made new friends from Japan, Singapore, and France who joined her in singing the birthday song and eating chocolate cake with green turtles swimming across a sea of white frosting. The birthday gaiety was a nice complement to the spirit of Thanksgiving, which was right around the corner.

Simple errors in judgment often become the most memorable occasions. While at Johor Bahru, Malaysia, we were enjoying a culture show that included Malaya folk dancing until nephew David and I were coaxed to the stage by a lovely Malaysian dancer. I should have ignored her smile and the beckoning tilt of her head, but didn't. Fortunately, my niece had forgotten the video camera. I'd like to think optimistically that the missing camera will hasten a fading of this memory of Uncle Larry unceremoniously swaying with the rest of my adopted dance troupe. But families don't forget embarrassing moments, they dwell on them – talking and laughing about your misadventures even after you've passed to the Great Beyond.

Thanksgiving Day brought us a traditional turkey dinner at The American Club where we joined two other families for a gathering of 16 wonderful people—most of whom did not know each other before dinner. There was an American couple from Germany, my colleague John Smallman had his mother and father from Indiana, there was a young woman from the Philippines, a little girl from Japan, and diverse others. Nephew David said a good prayer and just like in America, we Americans ate slightly too much and talked about how many blessings we were thankful for. In listening to the dinner conversations, I learned that the fortunate events, all the nice things that combine to make us who we are, are really too numerous to count. All we can do is bow our head and say, *Thank you, Lord, for all that you do!*

My family returned to the United States the day after Thanksgiving. It was early, they were half-asleep. I was grateful for the time with them and most especially to be with the children. Children wear us down, but in doing that they build up our best part, the human heart.

Polynesian Paradise

Scotsman Robert Louis Stevenson (1850-94) was an adventure writer who loved travel. Born with ill health, during most of his short life he fought the handicap of tuberculosis. Millions of people around the world have enjoyed his books, *Kidnapped, Treasure Island* and *The Strange Case of Dr. Jekyll and Mr. Hyde.* I was reminded of his talent and life on a recent visit to Upolu, a Samoan island in the South Pacific. Stevenson was much loved by the Samoans who called him Tusitala (teller of tales). From 1889-94, he lived at his 314-acre plantation on a promontory overlooking the Pacific.

Samoa is a remarkable country that blends Polynesian culture with the influences of German and New Zealand colonization and the Christian zeal of missionaries. Today, the islands of Samoa have 160,000 inhabitants (another 160,000 expatriates live in New Zealand). Nearly 100 percent of the people are Christians who devote Sundays to worship and many individually observe 10-20 minutes in an evening prayer ritual every day.

Tattoos are part of their culture and they love to sing, make music and eat well. Both male and female Samoans are among the largest people on earth. One of the heaviest Samoan women was Pii Moamanu who, when she died at age 38 in 1931, was 6 feet, 7 inches tall and weighed 518 pounds. Last year, my colleague Corbin Rinehart and I were on an assignment at the nearby Polynesian Kingdom of Tonga where Corbin asked the police commissioner what he thought the greatest threat would be to US sailors during a ship visit. The commissioner thought a moment and responded with a grin that in his view the greatest threat was that one of our young sailors would offend one of his young ladies and she would beat the crap out of him. Size matters!

The Samoan islands have beautiful beaches, clean water, and refreshing ocean breezes. The interior is mountainous and a canopy of rainforest covers much of the area. It isn't easy getting there. In taking the most expedient route from Singapore, it took me 22 hours to travel the 7,000 miles. Hawaii is closer; it is just 2,400 miles northeast. This isolation means that Samoa doesn't change much, there aren't many tourists there and those who do make the trek are truly serious about being there. The Australian Overseas Aid Program is actively helping the Samoan police better serve their communities, particularly in improving protection for women and children. There are also 56 U.S. Peace Corps workers helping in community development, the United Nations has a contingent working to improve education, and the World Bank has a program to increase job opportunities. The country has nearly 370 small villages administered by councils of Samoan chiefs, 18,000 of these chiefs (heads of extended families) are registered with the government.

Over the past hundreds of years Samoa has been reached by beachcombers, shipwrecked sailors, blackbirders, traders, missionaries, explorers, soldiers, and those more famous in our own times. Some who have made the trip to Samoa are American author James Michener who visited often during World War II service. Later Michener published, *Tales of the South Pacific,* which won a Pulitzer Prize and was made into a stage play and the movie, *South Pacific.* Others who have visited are Gary Cooper who made the movie *Return to Paradise* there in 1953; and actors Marlon Brando, William Holden, Raymond Burr, Cheryl Ladd; and members of the British Royal Family.

During my five days at Upolu, I lived at Aggie Grey's Hotel in the capital city of Apia. The hotel traces its origins as a hamburger stand that served US servicemen during World War II. That's where James Michener met Aggie Grey, a larger-than-life personality who influenced his development of the character Bloody Mary in *Tales of the South Pacific.* Apia, with just 40,000 people and one of the most intimate and picturesque small harbors in the world, is an exquisite place. The people are relaxed, well-dressed, and polite complete with an aura of exemplary grace.

Two of my most memorable events occurred after sunset on a park bench beside the seawall on Beach Road. Sitting there with my beautiful friend Lemapu Wong, a Samoan man named Philip came up from the Small World Department to introduce himself. Wearing a broad smile he was pleased with his powers of observation and wanted to tell me that he had seen me jogging at Tonga last summer and also seen me running in Apia a few days earlier. My lesson here is that we often don't know who is watching and how these casual observations may come back to us in the future. The other event was three women sitting down at a nearby park bench and serenading those nearby with romantic Samoan ballads in three part harmony. They should have been on a stage with lights, cameras and a crowd of thousands, but instead they were singing for their love of harmony. The South Pacific is renowned for song and it was my lucky night.

One of the features that make Apia a standout community is the abundance of church steeples and stained glass. On my one Sunday there I attended the white wood-framed Apia Protestant Church. It was founded by the London Missionary Society in 1849. I arrived 15-minutes early on a warmish morning, but there was only room to squeeze into the packed pews. The youth choir was singing and the lady parishioners all had a hand fan in vigorous motion. A lazy black cat strolled beneath the pews seeming to touch every leg and overhead fans were spinning energetically sending a cooling breeze that didn't reach far enough. When the service started the youth choir was replaced with the adults, who were also uplifting in expressing their passion for Jesus. Regardless of whether you're a Christian or even enjoy attending Sunday services, having the opportunity to hear a Polynesian church choir is not to be missed.

Robert Louis Stevenson had the heart of a poet and created a body of work that included poems of love and verses of praise for God in a small prayer book. It's interesting how good people attract and remember one another. Stevenson was highly honored in his lifetime by the Samoan chiefs and today his memory is part of the historic charm that separates Samoa from the rest of the world.

Land of Smiles

Fifty years ago, Margaret Landon wrote a novel so acclaimed that it was made into a successful screenplay, and then transformed from stage to the movie screen. The story of Anna and the King of Siam, set in the 1860's, featured a British tutor who brings western influence to the royal family in what was Siam (country name changed to Thailand in 1939). Anna and the King continues to be of interest to us because it shows people struggling through differences, learning to change and coming out better in the end. The book, play and movie conveyed a sense of exoticism that exists even more in the real life setting of Thailand.

Two weeks ago, I was in the Kingdom of Thailand on business and a state of awe over the splendor, irony, and the wonders of human behavior. As a primer: Thailand is a country of 62 million people, 250,000 of which are Buddhist monks. The monarch is King Blumibol Adulyadej who will celebrate his 77th birthday on December 5.

The country receives about six million tourists a year. The reason people flock to old Siam is for scenic beauty and because the Thai people believe life is fun in all things from eating to strolling with friends. They start conversations with a smile, seldom raise their voices (that happens to be rude in Thailand) and in lieu of a handshake they put their hands together and bring them near this chin and give a slight downward tilt of the head.

The country inspires wonder – everyone says that. Most boys spend several months as monks, it's a major rite of passage, but not many women become nuns. That said, later in life women often dedicate weeks to living at Buddhist temples to pray and assist the monks with the laundry, cleaning and food preparation.

Two things that make Thai people angry are to show disrespect for the king or disrespect toward Buddhism. The country borders Burma, Laos, Cambodia, and Malaysia. Good things there are kick-boxing, kids, kite flying, elephants, tigers, monkeys, orchids, jasmine, rose apples and other fresh fruits, beautiful beaches, mountains, rainforests, and obviously, kindheartedness. The rubies are nice, too. Over 70 percent of the world's rubies come from Thailand.

On the nasty side we find bird flu, drugs, HIV/AIDS, a few terrorists, wild boars, sex offenders, and snakes. If I could tell one story that best captures the spirit of generosity that is Thailand it would be last year's announcement by the Thai government asking that countries stop sending foreign aid and that funds designated for Thailand should be sent to neighboring countries with a greater need.

My time was spent at Pattaya, a resort community on the eastern seaboard. This beach town of 65,000 is the epitome of neon, go-go, and transvestite shows. It was once the proverbial sleepy fishing village, but during the Vietnam War it became a rest and recreation center for US servicemen. Some have returned, but now have 50-inch waistlines, faded tattoos, graying ponytails and a passion for motorcycles. Be that as it may, most male tourists are from Japan, Australia and Western Europe. Walking past the beer bars, massage parlors, and discos, there is a sense of economic principle at work with sex starved (or is that crazed) males providing a form of income for rural women who otherwise would find it more difficult to support their families. My sense of it is that beneath the glamorous make-up and fake smiles no one, man or woman, are particularly happy about their circumstances.

With this worst part of Pattaya explained, the area also has family sports, cultural shows, game fishing, scuba diving, elephant treks, a spectacular tiger zoo, and historic temples.

My most vivid memories occurred in unusual settings. One morning I was walking near an isolated munitions pier and as I started to cross a small bridge a co-worker pulled me back with the admonition *snake!* And sure enough looking down I saw what I later learned was a red tail natter, a nonpoisonous (but bite happy) tree snake that grows to seven feet. It was about a foot from my right hand. Those kinds of experiences take my breath.

My other great moment occurred as I watched Aim Sin paint. She was a creative elephant at a culture show I attended to watch elephants play soccer, basketball, bowl, make music, dance and paint pictures. Her picture is now framed and hanging at home. It is a handsome rendition of a flower garden and is better composed than some of the human handiwork I've seen.

Anna and the King of Siam, published in 1944, was based on the life of Anna Leonowens who died in 1915 after writing extensively about her experiences as an English teacher for the royal family. Unfortunately, some of Anna's facts were not factual and resulted in offense to the King. That made the Thai people mad – remember the two cultural no-nos: disrespect to Buddhism and disrespect for the King. Margaret Landon, author of *Anna and the King of Siam*, and her husband served as Presbyterian missionaries in Bangkok for ten years where she researched Leonowens' experiences in Thailand. She was also principal of the mission school at Trang. In sixty-seven years of marriage, she and her husband raised four children. Margaret went to heaven in 1993. If she were alive she'd still be pleased with what we find in Thailand today, but we wouldn't let her go to Pattaya!

Christmas at Sri Lanka

Because of my experiences I don't need to be reminded that the most important events in our lives revolve around relationships: sisterhood, brotherhood and fellowship among mankind. Humans are beautifully unique in the love they have for one another.

It is the mother and child, dads and kids, men and women, husbands and wives, boyfriend and girlfriend, little ones and their grandparents, and strangers who come together for seconds to make eye contact and share a smile. Humans also love their pets, sometimes more than people; we love nature, food, and substances that alter our moods – sadly, we sometimes love these too much with a resulting misery, but it is a happy heart that gets us there. I like this thing love, the passion that goes with it, and extending us toward the edge. And don't you think it plays an emotional crescendo in December as the Christmas season envelops us in its nonsense and magical lift? The sentimental music—our favorite carols, bright colors, fabulous food, and a sharing of excitement with children bring us all closer if only for a few weeks.

The Christmas month took me to Sri Lanka and there were even a few days to be in my beloved Singapore. I learned a few things in these travels and as with new experiences in meeting people, seeing things or even reading books, we are never the same later. Little by little we change from our experiences and with the grace of God these will be good changes.

Sri Lanka is an island nation off the southern coast of India. It has 18 million people who reside in a paradise of beaches, rainforest, and mountains. It is a gem capital of the world with topaz, rubies, sapphires, and emeralds all there in the ground to find and polish up.

There are elephants, porcupines, wild boar, cobras, tea estates, cashews, stiff ocean breezes, monsoon rains, and pleasant people. Sri Lankans are a people extracted from India, Portugal, the Middle East, and the United Kingdom. They are Buddhists, Muslims, Christians, Jews, and Hindus. If you are wearing clothes, there is a good chance that they were manufactured in Sri Lanka. The country also does light manufacturing in electronics and my Singaporean friends tell me that the best tea in the world comes from the highlands of Sri Lanka.

While on this trip I continued my relationship with Majid and Leena Awn. They are business colleagues and a delightful couple. They are also Muslim and what caught me unawares was their enthusiasm for the brotherhood that Christmas brings. For years they have hosted a large Christmas Eve reception at their home for friends and family members who represent all religious faiths. Majid told me that that is the situation in Sri Lanka. Everyone celebrates everyone else's religion on special occasions like Christmas. His view is that families are so cross married into different ethnic and religious communities that they can scarcely say anything bad about anyone's belief without offending a relative. That's brotherhood!

Of course, not everyone gets along. The Tamil Tigers, an international terrorist organization instigated a 20-year civil war that is just now winding down with a loss of 100,000 lives, many of them women and children. I also met Sasa Gao, a Chinese student studying English there. Sasa doesn't get along with tuk-tuk drivers. Tuk-tuks are small three-wheeled conveyances that transport two people helter-skelter over short distances. When I met her she had only been in Colombo, the capital, for five weeks and had been assaulted twice. On both after-dark occasions, the driver was after her purse. Showing me the bruises from her second attack she proudly used her evolving English skills to explain that she had beat the crap out of the second driver. Sasa is tall and fit and she didn't want to lose her purse a second time. Okay, I agree with Sasa that not everyone gets along that well at Christmas and petty criminals don't fit into my idea of brotherhood either.

On a free day from work, John Smallman, my traveling colleague and I took a day-trip to the elephant orphanage at Pinnawala, 45 miles from Colombo. It was my first time to even consider that such institutions existed, but this one has been around since 1972. It was started as a crusade to save as many elephants as possible, especially those who have been orphaned; there are now about 2,000 Asian elephants wandering around Sri Lanka where they are progressively becoming a nuisance. Problem is that the wilds are shrinking as people take over more land for coconut, rubber and tea plantations. The elephants require two acres of foliage a day to live and they wind up snacking on private property. My thought is that these snacks are probably notable, which gets us human's angry.

At the elephant orphanage we sat with hundreds of other people on the river bank watching about 60 elephants—many babies—bathing and playing in the Maya Oya River. It was mesmerizing as they patted, pushed, sprayed and gently shoved one another. It seems that elephant's have a great affection for their brothers and sisters just like people. Besides the toddler elephants, a star of the show was an elephant that had its right front foot blown off by a landmine (remember the Tamil Tigers!). There was another elephant that had been blinded by a shotgun blast in the head.

In Sri Lanka as in Singapore, Christmas is a festive time regardless of religion or ethnic origin. Because of religion not every Sri Lankan appreciates the meaning of the Christ child, but many Christian's don't either. Several years ago, humorist Garrison Keillor wrote an essay on Christmas that suggested Christmas was about bright lights, good food, and friendships and that gifts should be in the spirit of macaroni and cheese dinners, postage stamps, and underwear. I don't recall that Keillor mentioned celebrating the birth of Jesus. Perhaps it's enough just to love each other in the spirit of Jesus as we exchange lighthearted thoughts and macaroni and cheese dinners, postage stamps, and underwear. Using the model of brotherhood in Sri Lanka might be a good start (minus the terrorists)!

Life Goes On

In 1975, many people watching a movie became terrified of going into the ocean and it still has the same effect today. The movie *Jaws* was a work of fiction created by Peter Benchley. It starred a deranged great white shark that had developed a large appetite for humanity. Thirty years later many people who watched and lived through Asia's tsunami also have a sense of terror about the water and the awesome power of nature.

Early on Boxing Day 2004, there was a random act of nature involving a grinding together of the Burma Plate and the Indian Plate (there are seven major plates and a few minor ones that touch together in making up the earth's shell) that resulted in a slippage of 50 feet and a break on the edge of the Burma Plate that extended about 750 miles. This happened 18 miles below the ocean surface. Normal slippage is about 2.5 inches a year. The earthquake that followed registered 9.0 on the Richter scale. Earthquakes can only be measured on Richter up to 9.5 so this was one of the biggest. Scientists say it was the largest earthquake in 40 years. This huge sudden movement displaced billions of gallons of water and started a watery reaction that sent long waves on a speeding course toward whatever landfall they would encounter. Eleven countries were eventually struck by the tsunami. Indonesians on the island of Sumatra suffered worse because they were doubly affected: the nearby earthquake and the tsunami. Ultimately the death toll surpassed 200,000 people from 48 countries.

Because of our wondrous technology in mobile telephones, digital cameras, Internet, and television, most of us are now equipped with new knowledge. We can pronounce tsunami and several Asian place names; we know significantly more about geography and the natural processes of geology; we've learned about Asian governments, politics, rebels, terrorists and separatists. Religion is important in Asia and we improved our knowledge about Buddhism, Islam, and Hinduism. Stories of heroics and the ironic circumstances that spared lives will inspire and intrigue us for years into the future.

For some there is a new belief in God, others are more respectful of the ocean. Those who witnessed the terror by losing everything they owned or loved or lived for can't be totally put back together. The survivors cried in despair or were disbelieving not wanting to give up hope. We learned about tropical vacation spots so beautiful and warm that people will fly 15 or 20 hours from their cold winter climes to reach them. Our global community became more intimate because of these images and we were reminded that everyone in the human family is vulnerable---rich, poor, brown, white, young, and old— everyone sheds tears and hurts alike. When one of the Muslim extremist clerics said that God was punishing the Indonesians for not adhering to extremist lifestyles none of us believed that—hopefully the cleric didn't either. God doesn't work that way – His influence is on the heart and mind to make us better people – mass murder isn't part of that process.

I recently finished the book, *Everything Happens for a Reason* (Harmony Books, 2004) by Mira Kirshenbaum. Kirshenbaum is a Ph.D and psychotherapist who has done her share of researching and thinking through her subject. It's good that the world has deep thinkers to help us clarify life's difficult issues. Dr. Kirshenbaum says that every tragedy provides either a gift or an opportunity. That doesn't mean tragedies are good or that we should pray for bad things to happen. On the contrary, her premise is that events have meanings. We can make them negative or we can think positive and look for the good that will result. If we do that with the Asian tsunami we immediately see that the world family has been brought closer together in a humanitarian spirit.

After years of being fragmented, it is refreshing to see so many pulling together for a common good. People are exercising extraordinary generosity by giving and grieving for strangers. As a result, poor people will have the opportunity to rebuild their lives with new schools, hospitals, mosques, temples, and homes. Some who didn't have children will adopt to give youngsters love and positive new directions. God will win converts and other survivors will change their direction by moving toward spirituality. Another one of the Muslim extremist clerics (Abu Bakar Bashir) expressed disappointment that the US and Australian military were received in Indonesia as guardian angels. He says he's losing the battle for the hearts and minds of survivors because of the humanitarian assistance. It's more likely Bashir is losing hearts and minds because he's on trial in Indonesia for terrorism.

While on recent business travel I had the privilege of working and living among the angels of Australia. With just 19 million people they are the number three donor country with a pledge of one billion Australian dollars. Throughout the towns and neighborhoods I visited, everyone was donating privately to one charity or another. It is the same in America where three small children in Monroe, Michigan, raised $321 for tsunami relief. They did it by having their mother bake cookies that they sold around town. The baker was my niece Lea Ann Nichols and sales staff consisted of her children: David, 12; Ashley, 9; and Erin, 6. I know what they did is being repeated by thousands of other kids in many other countries. On the sidewalks of Singapore, youngsters are out with collection canisters to buy school supplies for children in Sri Lanka. In donating, contributors also sign a card that will be delivered with supplies. When the hearts of kids are affected positively by something that happens thousands of miles away, it is a good thing.

On the emergency response front, we see that the United Nations is really quite good at disaster relief and that Save the Children, Care International, Doctors Without Borders, World Vision, The Salvation Army, the International Red Cross and hundreds of other nonprofit agencies are filled with remarkable people devoted to an important mission. Medical teams from Singapore, Japan, Australia, China, USA, Canada, Belgium, France, Germany, Chile, Switzerland and Israel have been working to ease suffering. There are 37 donor countries; they have pledged nearly seven billion dollars. The three top contributors are Germany, America, and Australia. The US helped in other meaningful ways. Besides cash and supplies, the USS Abraham Lincoln was in the vanguard of a 24-ship task force supporting Operation United Assistance. The 15,000 sailors, airmen, and marines delivered 2.7 million pounds of relief supplies and shuttled people and material with over 50 helicopters.

The tsunami wasn't a movie; it was the real deal that disasters are made of with the runaway laws of nature dishing out just about more than we could take. Be that as it may, just as moviegoers learned after watching *Jaws,* life goes on and what we make of our new beginnings depends upon us.

The Land Down Under

I recently spent three weeks on business travel in Australia. In taking the trip I felt like I was following in the footsteps of Ginny Kibler. Ginny is a friend from Washington, DC, who has several college degrees, casually reads stacks of good books, and is extremely wise. Ginny believes that she needs to get away on long trips at least annually to find herself. That's what she says, "I need to find myself." One year Ginny went to Australia for a month. She went diving at the Great Barrier Reef and strolled through caves to look at Aboriginal art. Ginny backpacked and stayed at hostels while I stayed in upscale hotels that cater to the business community. Even though I didn't follow her path exactly, we breathed the same air, and saw some of the same sights.

My travels started in Darwin, progressed to Broome—both in the north, before going to the southern cities of Perth, Bunbury, and Adelaide. The trip concluded on the island of Tasmania at Hobart. Ginny talked about Aboriginal art as being the highlight of her travels. I liked it, too, but there were other things that caught my attention.

In Darwin, I took a cruise on the Adelaide River with about a hundred other tourists. As luck would have it, there was a random drawing and I won the privilege of dangling two pork chops on a rope over the side of our boat. They were the largest pork chops I had ever seen, but they need to be that way to attract the attention of a passing crocodile. I dangled okay, a croc jumped four feet into the air to grab what was probably a light snack. These are saltwater crocodiles that can grow to about 25 feet in length, have inordinately large mouths, powerful jaws, and big teeth—the combination is lethal. I saw a dozen crocs up close during the 3-hour trip, which caused an initial thought that Earth would be made better if they were on

Mars. I still believe that. In Darwin, Paul Patterson, a business associate with the Commonwealth Government, told me that tourists had taught the crocs to jump so that they now leap out of the water to nab fish that fishermen reel into their little aluminum boats. I wanted to believe Paul, but knowing of the storytelling prowess of Australian men and women I didn't buy off on it. Besides, I didn't want to be accused of teaching a croc to be any peskier than it already is.

At Broome, I rode a camel at sunset on Cable Beach and through nearby sand dunes. It was my first camel ride. Camels are nicer than crocodiles and although they can be bite happy, I think we can peacefully co-exist. Not everyone knows that Australia is an exporter of camels—that was a new insight for me. They are captured in the wild interior of the country, broken and shipped off to the Middle East.

Cable Beach is a hangout for nude sunbathers, but I didn't know that either. The next morning, I was jogging there at 6 am, the sun was up, and it was getting warm—the temperature eventual reached 40C (104F). Head down, determined, and enjoying life, I ran past the rear of a van parked on the beach. I was awakened from my concentrated state by a thrill female voice, *If you please, don't disturb my privacy in the future*. Looking to my left, the van's back doors were open, the seats laid down, and a large naked woman was comfortably soaking in the sun's rays. It seems that I wasn't paying enough attention to my environment and this sunbather wanted to make sure I didn't miss anything.

As I ran further up the beach there were several dogs, more camel riders, and a naked man. He was walking briskly in the buff, not too proud, but also not afraid to publicly let it all hang out, so to speak. Later I wondered if Ginny had visited the nude people of Cable Beach. Before leaving the area, I bought cultured pearls. Another revelation; 60 percent of the world's cultured pearls come from Broome. Apparently, the water quality, nutrients, and temperature give oysters the homey environment they need to maximize production.

Another first occurred in Perth and it was one that Ginny would have missed. People who stay in hostels don't usually have elevators. At the Duxton Hotel on the banks for the beautiful Swan River, I got stuck on an elevator for 30-minutes. It was a disappointing experience as my expectations of a five star hotel is higher than finding myself situated between the second and third floors for more than a few seconds. Sitting aside the faulty elevator, Perth is a beautiful city, the river is lovely and anyone within a thousand miles of the city should plan to visit.

At Bunbury, I had an exquisite time jogging through the town's large wetland park. In the marshy landscape, I saw large black swans with bright red bills, there were also pelicans, storks, and hundreds of baby ducks. The sound of these birds and the chance to see them in their natural world was a never-to-be-forgotten experience. It's the kind of exposure that Ginny would ooh and ah about. The birds of Australia are striking. I love, as everyone does, the neon blue, green, and red lorikeets—small parrots. My other favorite is the sulphur-crested cockatoo. They are large white birds with a lemon headpiece that gives them a showy air of class. It was also in the countryside outside Bunbury that I saw my first kangaroos in the wild. They were shyly snacking on grass in a field near the road. Male kangaroos can reach a height of six feet; the females are much smaller. They are timid animals, but if cornered can be ferocious. I was happy to keep my distance.

The people in Hobart, that's on the large island of Tasmania, have their priorities in order. They have both a Cadbury Chocolate Factory and the Cascade Brewery. It can be a chilly place so it's good to have a large supply of chocolate and vats of beer at your disposal. Although it was summertime when I visited, the temperature hovered in the 11-22C (53-73F) range. There was also a breeze that felt as though it had traveled from Antarctica, which is 1,500 miles south. Hobart, population

40,000, is on the southern coast of Tasmania, home of the Tasmanian devil, platypus, and penguins. The interior of the island is filled with mountains and large lakes, fishing is good—people also raise fruit trees and work in forestry. I don't know if Ginny made it this far off the beaten path, but because of the flora and fauna it is one of the most interesting locations on earth.

Ginny's fascination with Aboriginal art is well placed. It is the oldest continuous art form in the world. Some of the cave paintings are 40,000 years old and much of it can be accurately interpreted by modern Aborigine artists. Interestingly, one of the genres used by the Aboriginal people is the x-ray technique where animals are depicted through their bone structure. Besides being great artists, the Aboriginals can yodel and play the didgeridoo, an elegantly decorated wind instrument that has been around for about 60,000 years—there are a lot of old things in Australia.

The Land of Oz is about the size of the continential United States. It has just 19 million people—mostly friendly, generous and good hearted. The geography, geology, and flora and fauna comprise one of the richest and most unique set of natural wonders in the world. There are vast deserts, large tracts of tropical rainforest, mountains, rivers, thousands of miles of white beaches, and the Great Barrier Reef. It is so diverse that people become lost or others like Ginny find themselves. Being neither lost nor found, I am pleasantly struck with a better understanding and appreciation for this part of the human family and the place they call home.

National Chicken Month

Humans and chickens have been pals for a long time. We're so close in America that September is designated as National Chicken Month. In the world today there are about 12 billion chickens, twice as many as there are us humans. They are famous for having their own history, movies, restaurants, brothel, a designated spot on the Chinese horoscope, and their own little town. And there is Colonel Harlan Sanders (1890-1980), who perfected a Kentucky Fried Chicken recipe and marketing strategy that leaves the world craving our friend, the chicken. Today there are 11,000 KFC outlets in 80 countries where people fork over nearly 10 billion dollars annually to expand their waistlines.

I like chickens and might someday even enjoy having several with decorative plumage scratching around in the backyard. My first contact with chickens was at a tender age and wasn't pleasant. At my grandparent's farm in Southeastern Michigan, I was assigned annual clean up of the chicken coop where 300-400 large white Leghorns made their home. The cleanup took several weeks and involved moving the large winter buildup of manure and sawdust from the coop's floor to a manure spreader that would then distribute the foul smelling natural fertilizer across nearby fields. It was the #1 lousiest job I ever had. Speaking of #1 lousy jobs, as a US Navy recruiter in East Texas in 1970 my first female applicant was a 21-year old chicken plucker. She worked at a chicken processing plant at Center, Texas, and assured me that no one had a worse occupation.

Now so many years later as I travel through Asia and the South Pacific I see chickens and people getting on quite well together and it tempts me to give them a second chance.

My favorite setting for this is the Vietnamese Embassy in Singapore where several chickens with feathers of neon red, russet-gold, deep green and brown scratch around for worms on the embassy grounds. They tend to crow every now and then and keep about the right distance from visitors.

There are nearly 300 breeds of chicken, plus an infinite number of varieties, in the world. Araucanas is a South American breed that lays blue, green or pinkish eggs. It is also called the Easter Egg Chicken; Rhode Island Red is the state bird of Rhode Island. There are breeds from most countries of the world. They are all colors from solid black to solid white, and come in large and bantam size. Their feathers are short, long, and sometimes highly decorative. Personalities are as varied as those in our human family with ranges from calm and gentle to nervous loners and those who aggressively fight.

Chickens trace their start to India in 3200 BC where the original chicken, the Red Jungle Fowl, is still around. Last November, my nieces Lea and Ashley and I saw one running wild in Singapore's rainforest. It's hard to believe that 12 billion chickens trace their ancestry to this one pretty-colored bird, but that's what the experts say.

Having spent time around chickens I am tempted to think of them as dumb clucks, but such is not the case. In the 2000 movie, *Chicken Run,* the cast of bird brains outsmarted the Tweedys, a human husband-wife team planning to make them into chicken pies. There was also a brothel that commemorates our fair-feathered friends. It was called the Chicken Ranch (1905-73). Located at La Grange, Texas, it was an illegal establishment that derived its name from the customer practice of trading chickens for sexual favors during America's Great Depression. So that we won't forget the Chicken Ranch, in 1973, ZZ Top, the Texas boogie band had a top hit called *La Grange* that gave a beat to the Ranch's memory.

If you were born between February 4 to the following February 4 in 1933, 1945, 1957, 1969, 1981, 1993, or 2005, you are a rooster in the Chinese Zodiac. If this is you, it means you are a deep thinker, capable, and talented, which sounds nice, but read on... You like to be busy, are devoted beyond your capabilities and are deeply disappointed if you fail. People born in the Rooster Year are often a bit eccentric, and often have rather difficult relationships with others. There are 12 animals in the Chinese Zodiac. I am the free-spirited horse and although we also have our problems I prefer that to being a rooster.

Chicken, Alaska is not a boom town. In the last census they had a dozen people living there year around, but the chickenites live without telephones, electricity and central plumbing.

When you get sick, follow your mother's advice and eat chicken soup. Mother's have been prescribing chicken soup for flu and colds for decades. As it turns out, medical research supports motherhood's intuition that the nutrients in chicken soup help us through the doldrums of cold-flu. The healthy brew is made with chunks of chicken, green peas, potatoes, onions and other vegetables.

For the future we know that the Chinese will continue moving toward world economic dominance, oil will become an increasingly precious commodity, global warming and changing weather patterns will challenge us, and that chickens will be there helping us see things through. Don't miss the new Disney movie, *Chicken Little* about a little bird brain who saves the world. It will be released November 4, 2005.

Resiliency in India

There's no doubt about it, life in my corner of the world is interesting. Because of the changing scene of people and places there are no dull moments except when sitting around Singapore's Changi Airport for two days. That happened several weeks ago, but to be honest I did go home the first night to the comfort of my own bed.

Late the second day I rebooked on another airline to a different Indian destination to skirt around Mum. Insiders call Mumbai, Mum, it's also called Bombay, a name it had until 1995 when Indians changed many of their prominent place names to traditional names that they would be happier with. Problem is that many aren't happier and still call Mum, Bombay. But that's neither here nor there.

The reason planes weren't flying to Mumbai is because of the southwest monsoon that brings wind and rain from July through September. This time the rain gods chose to dump 990 mm (39 inches) of rain in one day, a record in the past century. If you're been to Mum you know that the city has a crumbling infrastructure. When you combine 990 mm of rain with 18 million people in a city with outdated sewers and pumping stations there is bound to be trouble. Water backed up and there was a mudslide, a thousand people died from drowning, stampeding, shock, and being buried alive.

Indians have a lot of problems and they are used to coping. During the same week one of their large oil platforms (Bombay High in the Arabian Sea) caught fire killing 11 and forcing the evacuation of 355 people; a terrorist bomb killed 10 people on the Shramjivi Express train bound for Delhi; and during a brief respite from the rain an Air India Boeing 747-400 skidded off of Mum's airport runway, no one injured, but the airport closed again.

Asian Indians are resilient, they survive and many overcome the disadvantage of being raised in a country where one billion people have stretched real opportunity beyond the breaking point. They do that through education and entrepreneurship. They also love living somewhere else. In America, 30 percent of doctors are Asian Indians, 25 percent of the small hotels and motels are owned by Indians. There are three million Indians in the USA; another three million visit every year. They excel in computer technology and science, practice the religions of Hinduism, Islam, and Buddhism; their languages are as diverse as their stature and skin color – Hindi is spoken by 30 percent of the population, the rest speak 200 other languages. The Indians have a tradition of being argumentative, that makes democracy particularly difficult because one voice of protest can slow desperately needed social progress.

Instead of passing through Mumbai, I flew to Chennai, which used to be called Madras. I like the name Madras better. After spending the night there, my journey continued to the State of Goa. Goa was a Portuguese colony until 1961 and the million residents there prefer to be called Goans, vice Indians.

They are more prosperous thanks to rich deposits of iron ore, a better education, and have one of the highest literacy rates (77 percent) in India. Tourists like Goa and they come mainly from Australia, Russia and other European countries. Tourism started there in the 1960s with the hippie movement. One of those hippies was Frank Marshall, now a Hollywood producer. In 2004, he returned to Goa with Matt Damon and crew for filming of *The Bourne Supremacy.* From the film's first 10-minutes there are wonderful scenes of Goa's fabulous beaches and colorful people.

Goa is also famous for Catholic Churches, temples and old houses. Saint Francis Xavier's body is preserved at the Church of Born Jesus, built in 1586. Francis Xavier is the most prominent missionary after the apostles. He worked in Italy,

East Indies, Philippines, Japan, China, and India. The miracle he performed that I like best is bringing back to life a little girl who had been dead for three days.

While in Goa, I had dinner with Lonnie Fernandes and his son Hayston. Hayston is a 10-year old sixth grader and for the past year I've been sending English children's books to supplement his school lessons. Our dinner, at Martin's Corner, a restaurant near my hotel, was a time to get feedback on the reading materials. I found that out and also that we both have a passion for fried rice.

I also enjoyed meeting Jehangir Taleyarkhan. Jehangir is one of the last 200,000 Zoroastrians found anywhere on the planet. Zoroastrianism is the world's oldest religion and now I am fortunate enough to know three Zoroastrians in India and Singapore. They are all industrious, honest and charitable—the three pillars in their religious teachings. Jehangir is a business colleague and through him I met his wife Marian Felicia and daughter Ava. I was impressed to learn that Ava has completed her freshman year at the University of Nottingham in the United Kingdom.

Most impressive—mother and daughter communicate daily on the telephone while Ava is away. I was staying at the Park Hyatt Hotel near the community of Vasco da Gama. One of the best people there was my waitress, Komal Dhone. She told me the same story about her mother, Suhasini. The Hyatt is a 12-hour drive from Poona, where Suhasini lives. Mom calls every morning and has for over a year. A few days later I flew to Kochi (it used to be called Cochin) and was staying at the Taj Malabar Hotel. Through an odd chanced of fate I met Arya Nair, who related the same story of her mother, Indira, who calls her long distance everyday to stay connected.

There is a theme to the human condition in India and it's not much different from other developing nations – there are ups, downs, and diversions. Most people are poor and working hard for survival and maybe an opportunity that will come their way, and they don't give up. When kids have the opportunity for an education they study hard, there are mothers and daughters who stick together and people who believe in honesty and charity. There are also people who talk too much and slow social progress. And instead of changing place names like Bombay, Madras and Cochin, politicians could better serve by making improvements to infrastructures that let people live through rainstorms.

Thanksgiving in America

America is the greatest laboratory of social experimentation in the world. Americans bring together ideas, faith, and free enterprise to pursue big and little dreams. Most of these aspirations come true if people don't give up. At times it seems that the great democratic experiment is like a giant rocket ship streaking out of control across an ominous sky, no one knowing where it will land. And there are times of stress when Americans seem to be on the verge of a nervous breakdown.

The U.S.A. is the place where more ethnic minorities come together than anywhere else. The most Vietnamese outside of Vietnam live in America; the most Italians outside of Italy live there, the most Koreans out of Korea, the most Thais outside of Thailand; and the most Puerto Ricans outside of Puerto Rico. As a matter of fact, you can go right down the list, country after country, and you'll find practically the same result. There are 34 million people living in America who were born somewhere else. This mixing bowl of languages, music and dance, foods, religions, and customs is a wonderful gift that people everywhere respect in Americans.

I was reminded of these things recently during the Thanksgiving holiday with my family in the Midwest state of Michigan. Michigan is a playground set up by Mother Nature so that people would have an expansive outdoor setting with plenty of rosy-cheek weather to match. During my first few days the temperature dropped from 18C (65F) to -12C (10F). The wind blew hard, there were tornado warnings, it rained, sleeted and snowed; but several days were gorgeous with bright blue skies and a warming sun.

Every day I renewed relationships with family and friends, ran, read, and got caught up on overdue shopping. My jogging course went from the village of Dundee, past the River Raisin, and through the nearby countryside. Sometimes the cold wind was at my face, other times I was driven by a tailwind. The horizons in Southeastern Michigan tell a story of heritage and the future. I saw old red barns, darkened winter woods, high church steeples, and tall grain elevators along with microwave towers that relay cell phone signals.

The country is now amidst a serious debate on its future involvement in Iraq. The tone is mostly respectful and straightforward. Democrats have a tendency to blame the Republicans for their shortfalls in planning anything, the Republicans blame the media for negative reporting, and the media believes they are being maligned. We listen closely because in political debate anywhere in the world the truth can be elusive.

Americans are also edgy about the economy. General Motors, the world's largest car manufacturer is making 30,000 people redundant, Ford Motor Company is letting loose of 7,000 employees, and Delphi, an automobile parts maker has declared bankruptcy and is asking 185,000 employees to take a 50 percent pay cut.

Economists see these events as normal in a global economy, but that doesn't make it any more acceptable to fathers and mothers raising kids and concerned about the future. Bird flu gets a lot of press, America is not prepared for a pandemic (wide spread disease) and won't be for several years.

The people in New Orleans are frustrated because their communities on the Gulf Coast are not being rebuilt fast enough and meteorologists are awed in having tracked a record 26 hurricanes in 2005. So far the US has contributed 22 billion dollars in disaster relief for six of these storms and more billions are expected to be spent in getting back to normal.

Just like other places, American's concern themselves less with national interests and more with family and neighborhood issues, those are the day-to-day ups-and-downs that have the most immediate effect on their lives. In my case, I was concerned about getting fat. Americans are big people, you see that everywhere. They get that way by eating too much. Restaurants serve extra large portions for a relatively small cost and not enough people exercise.

Meier's Food Stores does public service announcements in the media encouraging people to eat responsibly. I should have listened, but got caught in the Thanksgiving cycle: we give a prayer of thanks for our blessings, overindulge, feel guilty, pledge to do better, but often don't. For many people parts of this cycle occur again and again. My niece's husband Chris summed it up best with his Thanksgiving Day quote: "I feel like a boa constrictor that swallowed a goat." I didn't feel that bad, but suffice it to say all of the 14 people hosted by my sister Linda were full to the brim.

There are many failed high school students gilded around the edges with some redeeming factors. I am one of those. Whatever intellectual qualities I acquired from elementary school and junior high school was lost in high school. While others accelerated toward a successful life at one thing or another, I lost ground that had to be made up later. High schools are remarkable places where parents turn kids over to other kids to learn about life.

The lessons I learned from classmates centered on sociability: getting along well with others, thinking positive, and staying good humored. My class was so strong in sociability that after all these years we continue to be brothers and sisters of an expanded family that is uniquely our own. While visiting Michigan I hosted my high school family with pizza at the local American Legion Post in Milan. Few social events have been as satisfying. Your best friends laugh at jokes that aren't funny while encouraging you more than you deserve. My classmates do that and more: they alter the past to make it seem better than it was and tell each other how young they look when they don't. Such creative efforts at being polite fall into the category of bald-faced lying. Be that as it may, God is forgiving with middle-aged innocents who occasionally lose their footing.

The best part of travel is that the chance of making new friends is enormously increased. That's right, it you want to meet someone new go to a place different from where you usually hangout. That's how I met Bobby Stamatopoulos, a Greek who has been in America for five years.   Bobby works at the City Limits Diner in Tecumseh.

Allan Tran was a South Vietnamese Navy officer who sailed with his ship away from Vietnam in 1975 as the Communist's took control. Allan and his wife own *Paradise*, a Chinese-Vietnamese restaurant in Ann Arbor where their daughter attends University of Michigan; and there was Miguel Torres and his wife Olga Rodriguez, citizens of Uruguay on three year work permits living in New Jersey. He's a construction worker, she an accountant. They were browsing at a Cabelas outfitting store and I couldn't help meeting them, he had a joyous smile, she was enjoying him, and both needed someone to take their souvenir picture. After the photo shoot, Miguel couldn't help but make the smiling disclosure of how happy he was to be in America, what a great country it was and how much he loved the outdoors of Michigan.

Then there was Kim and Mai Ngan on United Airlines Flight 895 from Chicago to Hong Kong. The mother-daughter team was returning to Vietnam on their first visit since arriving in Chicago four years earlier. At that time, neither spoke English, but they studied, worked hard and are happily succeeding.

These people   are   tiny   parts of America's great   social experiment, they represent the part where dreams come true and as my 7-year old niece Erin likes to say: "You can be anything you want to be..."   Although I had planned just a few weeks' vacation with my family, the time was better spent than I could have imagined in learning a little more about the human condition and the world we live in.

Sleeping Around

There is something good to be said about the value of sleeping in your own bed. I learned that by sleeping around and what I've noticed is that my bed in Singapore is best for me. That may be another way of saying there is no place like home, but I am not convinced of that as my enthusiasm for large doses of travel is undiminished.

In the past month I've slept in 11 beds and a sleeping mat on the deck of a ferry. Some of the beds were 5-star quality, some were just a sheet of foam rubber, and the sleeping mat was the worse. Traveling through Malaysia, Indonesia and Japan I saw things and met people you would have enjoyed. I was also in tight spots that made work truly seem like work. Be that as it may, I have the best job in the world and am not the least bit interested in trading it off.

My 10-days of travel in Indonesia was one of the best adventures as I traveled from Jakarta to Manado, Tahuna, Balikpapan, and Tarakan. Manado is in the northern province of Sulawesi, a large island in eastern Indonesia. The city and province is Christian, but there a lot of Muslims and people with other religious beliefs living together in respectful harmony.

The area is in the Ring of Fire, a volcanic island chain spread across much of Southeast Asia. While jogging in

Manado I stayed close to the oceanfront because of the sunsets, sunrises, and refreshing breezes. The changes from light to darkness and the reverse were spectacular with iridescent shadings of peach, purple, reddish-orange and yellow in far off skies. Because there are several active volcanoes in the area I suspect that the sky picks up its spectacular coloration from the release of gases and dust particles.

A community of 400,000 people living in a relatively isolated part of the world, Manado attracts divers who find the coral formations, underwater caves, and sheer drop-offs to be among the most interesting in the world. One diver I spoke with was thrilled to enter an underwater volcano that was filled with gaseous bubbles. To each his own!

In Indonesia, the people speak Bahasa, sometimes English, and sometimes Dutch. The area was once dominated by the Dutch East India Company, which found the spices of Indonesia to be as valuable as gold in a world market desperate for food flavorings and methods to preserve meat. Cloves, cinnamon, pepper, vanilla, and nutmeg are still providing a nice profit to plantation owners.

While running I learned a new word in Bahasa. One evening as I ran along the Manado waterfront a woman called my name, *Larry.* I stopped, turned and spied a stranger. Asking how she knew my name, she replied by introducing herself as Julia and said*, I didn't know your name; I only say you are running.* Giving a weak smile and puzzled expression, I thanked her and resumed the trek. About 30-minutes later the incident repeated itself. This time, a portly gentleman sitting in a lawn chair called out my name. I stopped and asked how he would know my name. He gave the same response as Julia in that he only said I was running. Several days later I introduced myself to a woman at my hotel, The Ritzy, and she said, *oh, your name* *is Larry, it means running in Bahasa.* Mental fireworks exploded, my face filling with surprise and enlightenment.

I have a tourist mentality in a working world that requires me to keep moving and keep producing even when I'd like to stop and smell the roses. My travel itinerary required work at the small island of Sangihe. There are two flights a week from Manado to Sangihe and the one I booked was canceled because of bad weather. The next best plan seemed to be taking a ferry on the 150-mile trip. Second best plans don't always qualify for the appellation "best" and there are times when we should refrain from using the term. It gives a false sense of confidence that things will be okay. The ferry had a capacity of 1,000+ passengers in three classes of accommodation: 20 cabins (40 people) 2 open-bay sleeping compartments (400 people each), and room for several hundred people on deck using sleeping mats. While the small plane would have taken 45-minutes, the ferry was an 11-hour experience; and because it was festival time at Sangihe, the ferry was nearly filled. The only tickets remaining were for the third best (or worst depending on your attitude) accommodation.

With my sleeping mat in tow I watched with interest as lines were cast off, the sky darkened into night and the rain started. At first the rain came straight down, but as the wind picked up it was blown sideways. I bought a blanket for a small added comfort, but the wind blew it away. The small ship hummed with vibrations from diesel engines straining against head winds and rising seas. The pitching from high seas on a small ship means sick passengers who hurl. My niece Lynn is in her 6th month of pregnancy. She has written me about hurling so it is a term that I am familiar with. I wasn't aware of the epidemic of upset stomachs until I saw ample evidence in an early morning stroll around the ferry.

Arriving at the small port city of Tahuna at 6 am, my first appointment was at 7 am and there seemed little need to shower, shave or change into dry clothing. That assessment was made in the realization that there was neither time nor place. At midmorning after the early appointment, workmates and I checked into the finest hotel in Tahuna. The daily room rate was $7.50 and the rooms were exceedingly clean; however, they lacked toilet paper (there were no toilets), soap or towels (no hot water, showers or bathtubs), air conditioning, or television. The rooms did have a squatting pan, convenient hose for cleaning up, and a large bathroom basin filled with water. The 10-room hotel served wonderful sweetened tea and brown sugared rice for a midmorning snack and delicious coffee with homemade cookies in the afternoon. We checked out in the afternoon for return on the evening ferry.

What a difference 24-hours can make. The return ferry enjoyed calm seas and I was able to get the lower berth in cabin 10. I was also fortunate that the night was warm, but heat in the cabin was unbearable. Back to a sleeping mat on deck I looked up at the sky. The reward was a view of starry illumination that city dwellers seldom see because light pollution erases the night canvas. In the middle of the ocean there are no distracting lights to hide the power of twinkling stars, an underestimated source of awe and beauty. Sleepy when I laid down, the sight of thousands of blinking stars brought me wide-eyed appreciation for the divine touch. The ferry hummed again with the vibration of diesel engines, the salty sea breeze blew away cares, and a light-filled sky stirred the soul. When we get our souls stirred whether by God or another human being we know what it is to be alive and happy.

At the Manado Airport awaiting a flight to Balikpapan, I had the rare pleasure of meeting Nichelle Wagania. A dark-eyed beauty with an engaging smile, she personified charisma. As I introduced myself and gave her a US flag pin, my workmate Joe Brummund passed her another gift. It was a large stuffed doll that he had bought at one of the airport shops. Nichelle was only 4-years old, but well on her way to being a leading charmer.

During my Indonesian travel I met men, women, and children--Muslim and Christian. Invariably they were friendly and happy with an interest in sharing their lives as students, homemakers, fathers, mothers, and so much more. They were also curious about my view of them and their country, and what my life was like as an American living in Asia. It was pleasurable being with them and although their beds aren't as comfortable as my own in Singapore, the richness of Indonesia's natural world, language, and personalities left a good impression that won't be erased.

Travels in Bali

Yesterday I returned from four days in Bali, Indonesia, where hundreds of red and white national flags were flapping briskly in offshore breezes while schools, storefronts, and parks dazzled the eye with red and white bunting.

August 17 is Independence Day for the Balinese and other Indonesians in remembering the country's inauguration in 1945. Not many American's visit Bali, but it has been in international headlines on two occasions in the past several years. As bad luck would have it Islamic Extremists traveled surreptitiously to Denpasar, Bali, to target tourists. Using their weapon of choice, improvised explosive devices, they killed 200 tourists in an attack in 2002 and in another assault in 2005, 22 people were killed. Be that as it may, Bali is the major tourist attraction in Indonesia and although the country is predominately Muslim, Bali is 95 percent Hindu. With a population of 3 million, there are 700,000 tourists who visit every year from Asia, Oceania, and Europe.

I went to learn more about land and spice plantations. Besides being a magnet for tourists who love surfing, and trekking mountains and dense jungles, Balinese farmers are among the most productive in the world with three crops of rice annually from their uniquely irrigated rice terraces. Spices abound with cloves, tea, coffee, cacao, and vanilla being popular cash crops. My friends, Luh Susantini Dewi (Shanty for short) and her husband Komang Jhonitha Surya Dharma, had located several prospective properties for me to view near their home village at Singaraja in North Bali (population 100,000).

Arrival in Bali is always memorable because of the exotic sounds, smells, and sights that greet visitors. There is music from bamboo flutes and xylophones, light breezes that deliver the sweet smell of jasmine and frangipani, and the spectacle of smiling people in traditional dress. The Balinese are high quality, that is to say, they are friendly, generous, and kind toward strangers. Their behavior reflects the gentle nature of their religion. Further to the spirit of this tropical paradise (voted #1 island in the world by readers of *Travel and Leisure* magazine), is architecture, which is rich in the use of mythical creatures.

Traveling with a rented car and driver, my friends Shanty, Dharma and I drove north for three hours on a narrow two-lane highway that twisted and turned through mountains, past crater lakes, playful monkeys, and rice fields that varied in color from gold to dark green. The air was cool and the sky memorably blue. We passed small villages and saw hundreds of kids marching in their school uniforms in practice for Independence Day festivities. Far off we could see inactive volcanoes and kites that fluttered, bobbed and weaved with the wind.

At Singaraja, I visited the properties, which were remote and at an elevation of 6,000 feet overlooking hills, valleys and ocean. They were mountainside parcels and populated with hundreds of clove, coffee, banana, teak, cacao, and other trees. The better of the two had an irrigation canal. I liked them, but had difficulty visualizing a level spot to build a home. Further, when Dharma and I did economic modeling to consider feasibility the properties could not produce enough cash flow to justify investment risk. After sleeping a night on numbers I awoke disappointed, but thinking about new ideas. We humans are wonderful at ideas, they reassure, strengthen, and exhilarate us, later we sometimes find them frustrating as we try to make them work. Such is life!

The next day I jogged through the nearby community of Lovina, while several hundred fit people were preparing for a 5K race. They were warming up beside the black sand beach to lively sets of music and after every song people were awarded prizes for the best warm-up moves. I thought about joining the group, but seeing how young, strong and trim everyone looked I questioned my judgment and simply moved along.

Both Lovina and Singaraja are typical of Bali with flowers everywhere, mountains on the horizon, and impressive trees. I love the huge old banyan trees and the coconut palms which stand everywhere you look. From Lovina tourists can visit dolphins offshore from 6-9 am, see sharks and moray eels, go diving to see colorful reef fish or be like me, think about sharks and stay on shore enjoying the breeze.

After jogging, my friends took me to the Banjar hot springs, a series of naturally warm and hot pools that gurgle and gush from inside Mother Earth. Because my hotel didn't have hot water, I found the water refreshing and in good contrast to the chilly hotel shower. While at the hot springs I bought a handmade patch quilt. The quilter was asking $15, my friends said that was too much, I got a lucky price of $10. A short while later a similar quilt was offered by another seller for $9. My home in Singapore is reaching museum quality with folk art from Asian countries. The Balinese quilt being the newest acquisition.

After returning by the mountain road to Denpasar where my adventure started, I stayed two more days for jogging, reading, exploring, and generally enjoying life outside the fast lane. Denpasar is the capital city of Bali, has 400,000 residents and a fair sized colony of expatriate Westerners who live the good life of wind, earth, sky, and water. They build nice homes, play golf, have tea parties and swim. Their homes are of Balinese style with all the modern conveniences.

As I jogged along the narrow alleys and roadways in the native residential areas, I passed temples, heard daily prayers and saw the flowers, food, water and incense that people set outside their homes as a gift to the universal God. There were cute kids riding bicycles, flying kites, and playing games; thoughtful old men sitting quietly among themselves; and young girls giggling their way through neighborhood life.

105

Life hasn't been easy for the Balinese in Denpasar since the terrorist attacks because their livelihood from tourism has diminished. One young woman I spoke with was unemployed for a year following the 2002 bombings. As difficult as it has been they haven't given up faith in their religion, their families or the future. That is part of the charm the Balinese people bring to the world. They are understated craftsmen and women and incredibly fine humanitarians. If we have a choice in where to live our lives, it makes sense to me to find the best people in the world to be your neighbors. That's why Bali is at the top of my list of most livable places on the planet.

Asia Extraordinaire

Don't you love the way we give encouragement to one another? A month ago I was at Padang, Indonesia, a beautiful port city on the island of Sumatra. On a Saturday at midday I started jogging just as kids were getting out of school. Passing groups of boys and girls in neatly attired uniforms, I heard chats *Lari, Lari, Lari...* As they chanted the Bahasa word for running, I smiled with the thought of how little they realized. Padang is a lovely city. While other places in Asia use motorbike taxis, in Padang they have pony carts, which is charming indeed, most especially when it is combined with Dutch colonial and old Chinese architecture.

Besides Padang, work took me to Medan, the capital of North Sumatra, one of 33 provinces in Indonesia; and to Weh Island in the province of Aceh.

En route to Weh, we passed through Banda Aceh, which caused me to think about how quickly lives can change from harmony and happiness to dissonance, sadness and pure tragedy. Events occur, some manmade, others natural occurrences that leave us breathless. There are more ways for us to lose than I can think of: hurricanes and tornadoes, divorce, illness, death, accidents, tsunamis, earthquakes, volcanoes, job loss, suicides, emotional break-ups, floods, and becoming a victim of crime to name just a few.

Although there are no joyful places to view the scene of mass death, Banda Aceh is an especially unhappy location to see 2004 tsunami damage. Riding from the airport to the Ulee Lheue ferry terminal our car passed Aceh Besar, a mass grave of over 47,000 people. The trench is outlined by a masonry wall and there is a monument under construction. The grave is a half mile long.

We also passed Zainal Abidin Hospital. It is now refurbished (thanks to Germany and Australia) from terrible destruction. The director lost all of his patients, many staff members, and at home, his wife and children. All of them gone! To his credit, the director returned to work the day after the tsunami and oversaw nearly a year of clean-up (there was 3-feet of mud remaining), rebuilding, and restoration of medical services. The reserve strength some humans possess is phenomenal.

Leaving Indonesia I traveled to Phuket, Thailand. Phuket is a gorgeous tropical resort island, which was also the scene of horrific lost of life in the 2004 tsunami. At Phuket, I jogged at Patong Beach every morning watching the sunrise and thinking of what it must have been like to be overwhelmed by a great wall of water. The beach is now cleared, monuments built, coconut palms planted, and new hotels and stores constructed. Of course, the shattered lives of the resident families can not be rebuilt and it will be a generation before most of the painful memories fade. In both countries, Indonesia with Muslims and Thailand with Buddhists, I am touched by the resiliency in which we humans cope with disaster.

One day I took a cheerful diversion to the jungle with an elephant trek up the side of a mountain, past a stream and waterfall, everything breathtaking with natural beauty. My elephant was gleeful as she stopped for a drink and then spraying her passenger...playful, indeed! Phuket Island is a paradise in every sense from happy and hospitable residents to the resplendent handiwork of Mother Nature. It is the peace and beauty of the place that contrasted sharply with the violence of tsunami damage.

The life of my Thai friend Dokrang "Frean" Traiking recently changed dramatically. A resident of Phuket Town, six weeks ago she received a call that her sister Pun had been hurt in a motorbike accident; the girl driving was killed. Pun suffered a broken arm and leg and severe head trauma. She spent 11 days in a coma miraculously coming awake a month ago. Frean and another sister, Tem, are now restructuring their lives to give

Pun home therapy for not only her brain injury, but also to help her walk and regain the use of her arm. In visiting the family I know the tears that were shed in coping with the shock of this accident. As tragic as her sister's injuries were, they have galvanized Frean with an iron will to bring Pun back to full recovery. Her example teaches that in moments of crisis we can and do rise to the occasion. It happens again and again.

While at Phuket one of my colleagues, Scott Bernat, took me to the Life Home Project, a home for HIV positive women and their children. Most remarkable is that the residents continue the Thai tradition of greeting everyone with a smile. It was at Life Home Project that I chanced upon Nok's story. Her life is a reflection on Thai culture, human behavior, poor choices, and bad luck: She was not blessed with a happy childhood, later made misjudgments in selecting friends and husbands, had children and was exposed to HIV through a drug-addicted husband. There are six billion interesting stories in the world, not all of them are happy, but like Nok many people do eventually experience light and become better as a result of their difficulties. As with Nok, the key to finding the lightness of being is keeping a positive outlook and kind disposition.

For the past several weeks I've been in Mumbai (formerly Bombay), Goa, and Mangalore, India. In Goa, a former Portuguese colony and gorgeous beach country, I jogged past rice fields, coconut groves, small pastures, village homes, and cheerful people.

The white cat got my attention. It had one blue eye and one green eye. I wanted to believe seeing the blue-green eyed cat was lucky, but later developed a respiratory infection and fever.

While in India, we celebrated Mahatma Gandhi's birthday. He would have been 137 years old on October 2. If he's not your hero, he should be. Gandhi taught us simplicity and stood for non-violence. He showed us that the world is a family and that we're all children of one God. The leading figure in social justice, he lived a distinguished life of peaceful protest. The Dassera Festival was also held during my stay. Dassera is a joyful annual event that celebrates the triumph of good over the forces of evil. I appreciate the optimism!

At Mangalore, a small Indian city on the Arabian Sea, I visited the port that included not only the passage of commercial ships, but also 300 cattle and 100 peacocks enjoying the luxury of port life. The cows of India are protected and the peacock is India's national bird. It's the cows that caused the trouble and sparked rioting in Mangalore last week. The main issue appears to be that Muslims like to eat beef (but not pork), the Hindus love their cows and treat them with reverence. They also like to eat pork! The rioting received its jump start when some Muslims in Mangalore were shipping a truckload of cattle for slaughter. The interception by Hindus to save the cows resulted in rock throwing, arson, stabbings, destruction of private property, closure of commercial businesses, a curfew, and the jailing of 50 people. My travel partner Chris Leaden and I left Mangalore a day earlier than planned.

Outwardly, the people of Indonesia, Thailand and India are different from one another, but scratch beneath the surface and they are brothers and sisters in one human family. In reflection, I am reminded of a favorite expression from Thailand: *Samo, samo, only different* and that seems to say all that needs to be said about differences.

Heavy Hearts in Cambodia

Obviously we live in times in which much of what we hear, read, see, and feel goes against the grain of human decency. The incidents of wars, disease, poverty, and social ills can be shocking. Maybe it's always been that way. There is a sense of guilt that resides in each of us for one thing or another. Beyond the smallness of our individual beings there are large events that make the human family reel in shame from the sheer cruelty.

Before going to Cambodia I had read: *When Broken Glass Floats, First They Killed My Father, The Stones Cry Out,* and *Children of Cambodia's Killing Fields.* Cambodia, geographically placed with bordering countries of Thailand, Laos, and Vietnam on the Indochina Peninsula, can claim the distinction of having one of the saddest national histories of the 20th century. Between the years 1975-79, a communist-extremist named Pol Pot gained control of the country in an insurgency and revolution that ultimately cost the lives of 2 million people (about 25 percent of the population).

In heart rendering detail, memoirs written mainly by young women recount purposeful starvation, torture, and mass murder that was ultimately labeled genocide. In the books I read their stories were told through the eyes of kids 5-15 years old.

I was pulled to Cambodia because of compassion, my push to visit was work related as I traveled to the capital of Phnom Penh and the port city of Sihanoukville. In the capital city I did my job, but also visited the Royal Palace (they have a king and a democratically elected parliament), the Russian and Central Markets; the National Museum with Khmer antiquities 800-1,000 years old; Tuol Svay Prey High School (the country's main torture center under Pol Pot's Khmer Rouge); and the infamous Killing Fields at Choeung Ek.

There is a painting I bought on this trip that symbolizes what I saw and remember. It is a rural scene with lines of people stooped over harvesting rice, there is a bullock cart loaded with straw, and a pond with red-blossomed lotus plants. The pond and lotus remind me that during Pol Pot's insane social experiment starving farm workers survived a day or two longer by eating lotus seeds.

Today in Cambodia there is still little mechanization, so thousands of bullock carts and people spend an inordinate amount of time in labor intensive agriculture.

Pol Pot's nutty plan was to relocate all the city dwellers to the country to become farmers. He closed factories, discarded appliances and automobiles, almost everyone lost their home, ownership records were destroyed, and Buddhist temples burned. Because he didn't want a counter-revolution he targeted for extinction anyone with an education, i.e., government officials, teachers, soldiers, doctors, policemen, religious leaders, and people who wore glasses because they could probably read. Their spouses, children, and extended relatives were also marked for death. Further, Cambodia is now one of the most heavily mined countries in the world with an estimated 60,000 people killed by explosions since 1970; most of the victims were children and farm laborers.

Because of Pol Pot's unusual cruelty to people of Vietnamese descent, the Vietnamese Army pushed into Cambodia in 1979 to stop the bloodshed, Pol Pot's Khmer Rouge were pushed to the Thai border where they resisted for many years in an isolated area. Vietnam's 10-year occupation was harsh, but Pol Pot's forces didn't stop fighting until 1998. In 1993, the country had its first successful democratic election, but it was marred by violence and corruption, a characteristic of most elections since.

During my one week in Cambodia I talked with more than a dozen men and women, 40 years or older, who recounted in soft, reverent tones, sometimes on the verge of tears, the shocking experiences in losing family members and friends to starvation, disease, or worse. Many people simply disappeared. They were led off and their whereabouts unknown until the mass graves were found years later. To date, nearly 20,000 mass graves have been located at 380 sites around the country.

The most infamous and largest murder site is at Choeung Ek, a few miles outside of Phnom Penh. In what was a Chinese cemetery and fruit orchard, the Khmer Rouge buried about 16,000 people. Walking with head down, your eyes see teeth and human bones breaking the ground's surface along with remnants of clothing. Eight thousand people have been uncovered and their skulls displayed in a memorial that includes several incense burning Buddhist prayer stations. The skulls show evidence of being crushed by small caliber bullets, axes, hammers, hoes, and machetes. My guide could scarcely talk above a whisper, his throat in a knot. He started working at the site in 1980. The tour concludes by sitting in contemplation, which my guide and I did. He explained that Pol Pot was inspired by China's Chairman Mao, and he damned the Chairman; he continued that Pol Pot's murder of Cambodia's best people was for no good purpose and he damned Pol Pot. He was in tears and I swallowed hard.

Tuol Svay Prey High School, best known as S-21, was the torture center that supplied victims for the killing fields at Choeung Ek. Located at Phnom Penh, victims traveled through imprisonment at S-21, to be brutalized for information before being loaded onto trucks and sent to their death at Choeung Ek. It is also a memory to cruelty of the times with blood stains remaining on concrete floors along with instruments of torture and thousands of black and white photographs of men, women and children, who had their pictures taken upon entrance to the facility. The pictures are large, and you can see confusion, fear and innocence in the eyes of victims. My guide was Pen Phalla, who had lost her husband and a young daughter to the terror. The tour was solemn.

Events in Cambodia were memorialized in 1984's Academy Award winning film, *The Killing Fields*, which told the true story of Dith Pran, friend and translator to New York Times reporter Sydney Schamberg. Dith's supporting actor role was played by Cambodian doctor Haing Ngor, a genocide survivor who had lost his family to Pol Pot's revolution.

Cambodia is a special place for America, which is the country's major export partner. Most of the commodities sent to the US are finished garments. About 320,000 people, mostly women, work at 286 clothing factories where working conditions are good, but wages low at about 25 cents an hour. Through the U.S. Aid for International Development (USAID) the United States built the best highway in the country, the Friendship Highway that runs 136 miles from Phnom Penh to Sihanoukville and millions of more dollars are well spent each year on programs that improve democratic processes such as elections and promotion of a free press.

Human trafficking is a serious problem as thousands of children and young women are kidnapped, recruited, or enticed into domestic servitude or the sex industry (sometimes girls are simply purchased from destitute parents). The US and other countries encourage the Cambodian government to try harder to eliminate this social cancer. The US also helps with workforce training and youth education to better Cambodia's economic future.

Cambodia is a naturally beautiful country with lovely people. That said, it is also a sad place with memories almost too terrible to bear. As much as we might wish such events would never take place they continue to occur.

In Cambodia, 1-2 generations of people were killed, now a vast majority of the population is young and with that comes a rebirth of faith, hope and optimism. All of us on the outside looking in can promote that feeling with our good hearts and open pocketbooks to help with ideas that teach and give opportunities.

Margot Perot and The Salvation Army

It is the Christmas season and I am following my heart's desire, just where we should all be. In the evenings I stand on a street corner at the Heeren Building on Singapore's magnificent shopping mecca, Orchard Road. In my right hand is a small red bell, my left hand holds pieces of candy, I smile, say "thank you...happy holidays, thank you, happy holidays," and give candy to donors. This is my 10th year of helping poor people through The Salvation Army's Christmas Kettle. More than most years, I am reminded of how one person can change our path for the better.

From parents and teachers through the thousands of people we meet over the course of our lives we change, mostly for the better, because of the passionate people with the good ideas who surround us. My interest in The Salvation Army was perked in 1997 at a breast cancer benefit luncheon in Dallas, Texas.

I had the good fortune to be seated with Margot Perot. Margot is a relatively unknown personality who lives in the shadow of her billionaire husband, Ross, an American character and entrepreneur of the first order. As the story goes, it was Margot who took a thousand dollars out of her savings account as a loan to her husband so he could start a management services company called Electronic Data Systems (EDS). That was in 1962 and the EDS concept proved right for the times as in 1984 Mr. Perot sold his company for 2.4 billion dollars.

Strangers but for a few seconds, Mrs. Perot and I had the best time exploring topics of conversation from her husband's activities, he ran for US President twice, to my enthusiasm for jogging, reading, and writing. Finally, she said, *you know, this benefit for breast cancer is okay, but my real passion in life is The Salvation Army.* Mrs. Perot explained that she was on the national board of directors for The Salvation Army and that there was no better or honest charity, which did more to benefit the needy. As we came to the close of our delightful

116

encounter I promised her that I'd investigate helping The Salvation Army.

A few months later, in December, my daughter Mary and I rang The Salvation Army bell at a red kettle outside a supermarket in Vienna, Virginia. Young Mary shivered from a cold, snowy wind and we both sang Christmas carols. She was five and as children tend to be at that age, she was too cute for words. Money flowed into the red kettle; people smiled, and wished us Merry Christmas. Filled with affection for generous strangers who trusted Mary and me with their donations, I realized that helping the less fortunate best fit my idea of what celebrating Christmas should be about. In later years, friends and I formed teams and we had territories, relieving each other and always feeling the inner warmth of giving time to benefit down-on-their-luck people with clothing, food, and toys for Christmas.

Several years, I was on holiday vacation in Michigan, contacted the local Salvation Army and took up bell ringing just where I left off the year before except with an entourage that included a sister, nieces, and their kids. The spirit was always the same, not only mine, but the people who walked past taking a moment to drop whatever they could spare into the bright red kettle.

In January 1998, I wrote Margot to tell her about the experience Mary and I had with bell ringing, she responded with a lovely handwritten letter of congratulations and described her own experiences at ringing the bell in Dallas-Fort Worth. Later I jokingly told friends, *if I were Mrs. Perot, I'd just write a check for a million and go to the Caribbean for the holidays*. Obviously, I had missed the point. She gave of her time in spite of wealth and as a result realized a unique richness that we can only achieve by giving of ourselves.

In 2003, I started ringing the bell in Singapore at Lucky Plaza and Far East Plaza, and now I am posted to the Heeren Building.

All the locations are prime shopping areas for tourists and Singaporeans. Whether I like it or not, I am noted as an Anglo working for the needy people of Singapore. My best clientele are teenagers, who are generous in their spirit to give something, and Australians, Americans and Europeans who relate the bell and red kettle from Christmases past. Everyday someone stops to tell me it wouldn't be Christmas without The Salvation Army. I want to say the spirit of Christmas wouldn't be with me either, but I just smile and give a nod of understanding.

Americans have improved the world in more ways that anyone can count; however, The Salvation Army is not a unique American enterprise, it is a charitable organization of the Christian Church started in England in 1865. The entrepreneurs were Edwin Booth and his wife, Catherine. While Edwin, who designated himself a General, administered to the poor and ragged, Catherine gained support from wealthy patrons who gave to their financially demanding work.

Today's Salvation Army is broadly based on the roots of our human family. As a sampling, the Army is located in 111 countries using 175 different languages to administer colleges and universities (nearly 500,000 students), hospitals and clinics (over 1 million patients), Christian Churches, homeless shelters, addiction clinics, daycare centers, HIV/AIDS clinics, and disaster relief operations for hurricanes, earthquakes, tsunamis, and floods; and programs to eliminate sexual trafficking. There are millions of ministers, musicians, church administrators, employees, doctors, social workers, counselors, and volunteers like me who staff the red Christmas kettles. There is a link between each of these people and that is a love for humanity and an extreme enthusiasm to be involving in helping one to another.

None of us by ourselves is going to make a major contribution in changing the world, but when we band together for a common good purpose like benefiting the poor and ragged as General Booth started doing in 1865, our collective actions give faith, hope and optimism to millions. No gift has more power. Wherever you are you might consider calling The Salvation Army to see how you can be part of the team that is bringing improvements to the lives of millions. Thanks to Margot Perot that's what I did!

Christmas Around the World

Just a scant 20 centuries ago an event occurred that dramatically changed the world. As an improbable start to the Christian spirit a miracle baby was born in the most miserable of conditions. In a dusty and dirty stable, Jesus is given life amongst the sheep, cattle, and donkeys. Taking place in Bethlehem, we've all learned to love this story of a Christmas birth and the growth of the child who taught us our most enduring lessons of charity, kindness, and love.

Three wise men known as the Magi visited Mary and the Christ child with simple gifts: Casper brought myrrh, Melchior, gold; and Balthazar, frankincense. As this great story goes the three were Zoastrian priests and astrologers from Persia who followed a guiding star to Bethlehem.

A third (2.1 billion people) of those in our human family believes in Christianity, another 1.3 billion are Muslims and a billion more people believe in Hinduism, Buddhism, and Judaism. Regardless of religion all are inspired by the life of Jesus, for His choices, devotion, wisdom, and example of forgiveness. The several hundred thousand surviving Zorastrians (world's oldest religion) are especially touched by the inspiration that Jesus gave to the betterment of mankind.

But Christmas has taken on new symbols over 2,000 years. One of history's most lovable characters unwittingly became pop culture's icon for our commercial Christmas, a parallel course that lives in harmony with Christian reverence for the Jesus' birth.

Saint Nicholas was born in Turkey, the son of wealthy parents in 271 AD. Losing his parents at an early age, he filled his heart with a love of God and humanity. Building his life on a foundation of compassion, generosity and goodness (he reportedly gave his fortune to the downtrodden), Nicholas ultimately became a bishop in the Roman Catholic Church. There are two characteristics that distinguished his life: a love for children and an enthusiasm for secret gift giving. Exceedingly popular, after his death he was named a patron saint for pawnbrokers, bakers, druggists, judges, fishermen, thieves, the falsely accused, sailors, students, children, and merchants. *I emphasize merchants and children.*

About 900 years later French nuns started Christmas gift giving by placing food outside the doors of poor people on December 6, the anniversary of Saint Nicholas' death. The custom became popularly accepted in Germany and the Netherlands. Good ideas have always been spread person-by-person and it was the Dutch Protestants who popularized Saint Nicholas as Santa Claus as they migrated to the American colonies.

In 1823, what was to become the most famous piece of Christmas literature was released by a newspaper in Troy, New York. Clement Clarke Moore's poem *Twas the Night before Christmas* has since enchanted nine generations of children and parents literally around the world.

Developments started to go over-the-top in the 1830's with the commercial marketing of gift giving, and Christmas cards were popular in America by 1860. But it was not until 1931 that Santa Claus' appearance became uniform with a red suit trimmed in white fur and black boots. That appearance was introduced in a Coca Cola advertising campaign. *Remember that Saint Nicholas is the patron saint of merchants!* The story of our commercial Christmas is almost as fascinating as Jesus' birth.

Through this evolution the world has adopted candy canes, evergreen trees, bright stars and angels, blinking lights, fruitcake, nativity scenes, pretty paper and colorful ribbon, elaborate gift giving, holiday feasting and caroling as essential to a successful season. Fortunately, we have humorists who put things into perspective. The humor people are the educators and philosophers amongst us who teach truisms that bring a smile. My favorites are Will Rogers, Mark Twain and Garrison Keillor. While Rogers was mute on the subject of Christmas, Mr. Twain did have an opinion. It was his view that, ...*the approach of Christmas brings harassment and dread to many excellent people. They have to buy a cart-load of presents, and they never know what to buy to hit the various tastes; they put in three weeks of hard and anxious work, and when Christmas morning comes they are so dissatisfied with the result, and so disappointed that they want to sit down and cry. Then they give thanks that Christmas comes but once a year.* But, of course, Mark Twain passed from the scene nearly a hundred years ago.

For a contemporary take on Christmas we find Mr. Keillor a reliable witness to what we are experiencing. In his essay, *What I'm Giving You for Christmas*, he wrote: *It's a holiday fraught with peril. So achingly beautiful, with the lights twinkling and the choirs singing, and the glorious story about the Child and the shepherd's kneeling in the stable, and our hearts are open, full of generous and graceful feelings, but the dangerous urge to improve each other is overpowering at Christmas - the urge to give the family redneck a book about Western civilization, or give a makeup kit the size of a toolbox to a woman who has never worn lipstick in her life. Of course, these gifts are satisfactory to shopping malls and patron Saint Nicholas, but don't do much in bringing out the best in our family or friends.*

Keillor continues in his view that there is a perfect gift for each of us, but only we can find and buy our perfect gift, no one else can do that for us. When writing his essay in 1997, he envisioned the best gifts for anyone being white underwear, books of postage stamps, and packages of macaroni and cheese. He wrote, *these are simple and universal things, and giving them makes me a simple part of someone's everyday life, which is what I want to be. You realize as you get older that you aren't a wizard who can reach under your cape and pull out a magical object that will transform someone's life.*

I've always remembered his conclusion and I hope you will, too. Christmas is lights, food, and music with people you like to be with. It's about the wonderment in the eyes of children and opening simple gifts. When remembering a miracle Child's birth in a stable, there is an inner voice that suggests simplicity with compassion, kindness and love as being the best manner of celebration no matter how much merchants promote giving the perfect gift.

2007

Our Changing World

In 2004, my dad gave me five t-shirts for Christmas. They were from the University of Michigan and dad sent them to insure that I'd have a good supply of jogging shirts. After opening them I happened to look at the labels: *Made in Honduras, Made in Thailand, Made in Cambodia, Made in Vietnam* and *Made in Indonesia*. I found it ironic that none were made in America. For dad and I that was probably a good thing because if they had been made in America he would only have sent three shirts for the price he paid for five.

A few days ago, I opened a box of Kellogg's Frosted Corn Flakes, the company headquarters is at Battle Creek, Michigan. This is the same frosted corn flakes with Tony the Tiger on the box. While eating the crunchy flakes I started to read the back of the box. Tony the Tiger was there explaining something about soccer, but I become more interested in the languages. It was printed in Thai, Bahasa (language of Indonesia and Malaysia), and English. I read more; the cereal was made in Thailand.

In 2005, I bought land in Thailand for development of a rubber plantation. It is a new hobby and post-retirement career. Last year when my business partner, Wanvisa Techo, bought a tractor, it was an orange Kubota made in Japan.

Even though I am living in Singapore, sometimes on the Internet I listen to WAMU-FM in Washington, DC, through a process called streaming, it is my favorite radio station.

On December 31, my condo manager, Joey Li Mi, a 20ish Singaporean woman left to pursue her MBA at Boston University. I asked when she'd be back; she said that her plan was to stay in the US after graduating with work in Boston or New York City. Joey speaks Chinese as well as fluent English.

I have another friend in Connecticut, a Ph.D, who has a website www.succeedinAmerica.com, which benefits people needing advice on jobs and culture in America. A naturalized American citizen, Nara Venditti is a third-generation educator, born in Armenia and raised speaking Russian. Her business is booming!

I have a good friend and business colleague in Goa, India. His brother, Dr. Rusi Taleyarkhan, is a professor of nuclear engineering at Indiana's prestigious Purdue University.

A few years back, Jeff Brainard, an architect in Ann Arbor, Michigan, delivered twins at Mali, West Africa, while doing community service with the Catholic Relief Society. The dazed, but happy father literally gave Jeff the shirt off his back in gratitude. In the past four years, most of my new friends have been foreigners, their skin, language, and religion is different than mine.

These vignettes have to do with globalization and they illustrate a shrinking world as societies reorganize for the free-flow of ideas bringing people closer together. Thanks to the World Wide Web, digitalization, and the ability to transfer vast amounts of information in seconds, we're learning more about each other, finding things we like and things we don't understand. Our compassion is stirred when we learn about disasters like the 2004 Asian tsunami and our blood boils when Islamic extremists act without human decency.

Everyone reading this and billions more are reaping benefits from globalization. I live and work in Singapore, travel extensively and am up to my eyeballs in international thinking. I live at one of the important crossroads in the world. Singapore is a small city-country-island with just 4.4 million people and no natural resources except the brilliance of its people and government. Singapore traces its start as a trading post and now in the age of globalization it is continuing that tradition.

Commodities in Singapore's old days were fish, rice, rubber, opium, and spices, now the country is trading in the commerce of ideas, finance, deal-making, and setting an example for diplomacy and international friendship. Globalization is the migration of people, ideas, money, jobs, and commodities. It has to do with reducing the cost of research, manufacturing, services, and marketing. There are lots of winners.

American Apparel, a US garment maker in California pays its employees an average of $13 an hour plus benefits; in Cambodia, garment workers are paid $45-50 a month with few benefits. Needless to say, not many clothes are made in the US anymore because places like Cambodia, Sri Lanka, India, and China can make them just as well for far less. There are over 300,000 women making garments in new and modern factories in Cambodia. If those women were not making clothes for the world market it is likely that many would be victims of human trafficking. I am cheered that they are connecting with companies like The Gap and Levi Strauss who are giving opportunities to people who wouldn't otherwise be able to muster hope for the future.

We trace the start of globalization to an unlikely event: fall of the Berlin Wall, November 9, 1989. When the Wall fell liberating a captive people the balance of power shifted to countries that promoted democracy and free-market enterprise. It captured imaginations stimulating new markets and centers of commerce with smart people hungry for a larger share of the economic pie.

Other factors important to globalization have been the development of software that makes work faster and easier to manage, fiber-optics for the transmission of large blocks of data on the Internet, mobile phones, and large populations of well-educated and motivated people, i.e., India, China, and Russia; and large populations of underemployed, but no less motivated people in such places as Vietnam, Cambodia, Thailand, Indonesia, and the Philippines.

I like globalization, not so much because of the economics, but because it mixes us all up. Those with mobility carry culture, an enriching quality for people open to learning. By their example, the 14,000 Americans living in Singapore promote Western clothing, music, books, movies, Starbucks, McDonalds, and Famous Amos Cookies; but by the same token there are 33 million foreign born residents in the United States. They buy small businesses, introduce their food tastes, enrich our language, send their great kids to US schools and otherwise strengthen the cultural, economic, and intellectual fiber of America.

In Fairfax County, Virginia, my daughter's daycare provider was Shobha Khatri, a native of Nepal. When Mary started kindergarten there were 19 students in her class, only 3 had been born in the United States, the remainder were from Bangladesh, India, Pakistan, and a variety of Central and South American countries. The exposure from this rainbow of humanity enriched Mary's young life. I love my life overseas just as foreigners love living in America. Every day is an adventure, few things are ordinary, and I am learning something new every day.

What we are witnessing is only the beginning; globalization is like a rocket ship streaking across the sky with no one at the controls and a destination that isn't known. We do know that as different people come closer together conflicts arise; we see that behavior in our neighborhoods and along international borders. Humans have a tendency to love one another, but also fear those who are different. When there is a babble of languages, religious qualities we don't understand, new smells, different clothing, and gestures we're not used to there can be conflicts.

Crisis avoidance suggests that we exercise patience and not prejudge people or situations, that's called critical thinking and its part of what makes up a good attitude. I must do that every day or I would find myself isolated, confused, and unhappy in a foreign land.

Besides promoting harmony where differences exist, we also have a responsibility to encourage the next generation to think internationally for their own good. Instead of seeing ourselves as belonging to one nation, it makes sense to take ownership of the global community. Learning different languages, studying culture, traveling, finding foreign friends, and embarking on a road to study that exposes the world is the best course for any kid who wants to prosper and be well received in the years ahead.

Our children are the ones who will be making and receiving t-shirts in the future, where they are made and who uses them for jogging in what countries will be determined by economics and their enthusiasm to accept a changing world.

Congratulations and Be Prosperous

Congratulations and be prosperous! That is the theme of Singapore's Chinese New Year (Spring Festival), which is nearly upon us. It is now 4704 on the lunar calendar, but on February 18 it will turn 4705. That's also the date in which the good times roll for a 15-day celebration that sets the tone for future events. To help you navigate through thoughts of the Chinese and their New Year, you'll be seeing and hearing a lot about pigs. We are currently in Year of the Dog; they have just about had their final yap with the oinkers set to lead the way in 4705 or in 2007, if you insist.

Because the Chinese people comprise nearly 25 percent of the world population, when they celebrate it is a big deal. As an illustration, there are 33,000,000 Chinese living overseas (two million in USA); their New Year sets off the largest migration of people in the world as they travel home for reunion celebrations. The holiday is a mix of religion, traditional family values, and just plain fun. On the spiritual side, religious ceremonies honor Heaven and Earth, gods of the household and family ancestors.

And there are interesting customs. Ask a Chinese child about some of these traditions and their dark eyes brighten, they give a sweet smile and nod their cute little heads in joy. First, they are not to be disciplined on New Year's Day because there can't be any crying. Besides being noisy it brings bad luck for the year ahead. And secondly, it is their time to receive cash stuffed inside decorative red packets. The cash should be in even numbers for good luck. And lastly, the kids, parents, and rest of the clan are usually decked out in new clothes, the brighter the better. That also means good luck!

Getting ready for the Chinese New Year is no small undertaking because the home has to be thoroughly cleaned before the big day. Brooms, dust pans, and other cleaning paraphernalia must then be stored away because even accidental cleaning on New Year's Day could result in good fortune being swept out the door. Also, all debts should be paid and no foul language, bad or unlucky words, and negative terms can be uttered. That includes mention of death or dying and definitely no ghost stories. Oh, yes, no washing of hair as it could wash away good luck that has been building up for the year ahead.

The clicking of chop sticks in Chinese homes at New Years is a time for eating good foods in thanksgiving. Abundant traditional foods are prepared for family, friends, and deceased ancestors. Some of the things to load up on are lotus seeds if you want to have many sons; fish with heads and tails for togetherness; chickens with head, tail, and feet for prosperity and completeness; and noodles shouldn't be cut as they represent long life. One of my favorites is spring rolls, they symbolize wealth, and you should be glad about tangerines and Mandarin oranges as they mean luck and wealth, respectively. Just for fun foods at New Year are cakes, sesame balls, and almond cookies. Eating these treats promotes a *sweet* year ahead.

At New Year it is common to see lion dance performers moving to the throbbing beat of drums and counterpoint to gongs and cymbals. Because the lion is a holy animal in Chinese folklore, it is the perfect creature to create luck and drive away evil spirits. Two acrobats, usually boys, wear the elaborate lion costume, which is decorated with colorful strings, fringes, and tassels. Driving away evil spirits is no small task and it takes great young men to accomplish the task. The lion's paper mache head is expressive with eyes and mouth that give vitality to the climbing, dancing and jumping that the lion does in forcing bad spirits away. Lion dance acrobats and musicians are common sights at sidewalk performances, restaurants, hotels, and in shopping malls during the 15-day New Year celebration.

It is very fortunate for the couple that gives birth during the Year of the Pig. The baby will be fun, joyous, honest, and modest with a wide circle of friends. Pigs are also conservative creatures of habit that dislike venturing too far from home unless it is to the countryside. They love nature. People born in 1995, 1983, 1971, 1959, and 1947 are pigs. They are most compatible with rats, tigers, rabbits and dragons. You can instantly become an expert on the animal signs by research: visit a Chinese restaurant, read the paper placemat. Some of the famous pigs, and there is a long list, are Harry Lee Kuan Yew, Singapore's Minister Mentor, the Dalai Lama, Hillary Rodham Clinton, and Arnold Schwarzenegger.

In Southeast Asia, one of the most spectacular public celebrations of the New Year is Singapore's Chingay Parade that features thousands of international performers who prance in dragon and lion dances along with stilt-walkers, big-headed dolls, colorful floats, singers, musicians, and acrobats. The parade route follows opulent Orchard Road, which is decked out from sidewalk to tropical tree top with red lanterns and lights to encourage good luck in the year ahead. This year's parade will be on February 23 and 24.

You don't have to be Chinese to be part of the New Year fun enjoyed by a billion plus people. Like many celebrants around the world, they don't take all traditions quite as seriously as it sounds, but they like to remember the old ways on this journey we're all on toward the future. Remembering ancestors, enjoying friends and family, letting kids go wild for a day, eating good food and watching a parade, all good ideas. Congratulations and be prosperous!

Love Day

The earliest Valentine cards my family has are from 1910 and they were sent to my grandmother by friends. They are yellowed postcards with chubby cupids, purple hearts and simple sentiments.

My little boy orientation to Valentine's Day started with a card exchange in first grade at a one-room school house in rural Michigan. The small building held about 30 kids with studies in kindergarten through the sixth grade. The event was orchestrated by a great lover of children, teacher Mary Farrar, and didn't include the start of any sizzling romances. Much later I helped daughter, Mary, organize her first Valentine cards for young classmates in Herndon, Virginia.

From simple origins that date to the 1840's when America's first mass produced Valentine cards made a debut, we've sparked a winter heat wave of commercialism, joy, and sometimes resentment. We see corporate joy with card makers, candy and chocolate manufacturers, florists, restaurants, and jewelers. And there is more joy in people who are loved and find happiness in expressing the best affection for those around them. The figures on this affection are staggering: 180 million mostly red roses sold on Valentine's Day, one billion greeting cards sent worldwide, Valentine's jewelry store sales second only to Christmas gift giving, and a peak in chocolate sales (Americans consume 10-12 pounds of chocolate annually compared to Switzerland where individuals in that porky population gobble 22 pounds of chocolate every year).

The commemoration for hugging and kissing started with Saint Valentine, a Roman priest, who was killed February 14, 270 A.D., by the Emperor Claudius. Exercising his authority as a shaper of public policy, Claudius had decided that marriage wasn't in the best interest of Rome and banned it. Valentine defied Claudius by secretly marrying couples. It is worth noting that chocolate had not yet been discovered. It did not arrive in the Old World until Christopher Columbus returned from his exploits of the New World in 1492.

Of the one billion Valentine's cards sent every year, 84 percent are purchased by women. Men and women think differently. Shame on you if this is new knowledge! In the case of Valentine's Day, women think of sending an affectionate greeting to not only husbands or boyfriends, but also mothers, sisters, and daughters while most men only think to send cards to their wives or sweethearts. Many men also think that a little romance goes a long way as four times as many men as women feel pressured into giving a card or gift and they're a little grumpy about that!

Valentine's Day has a long tradition in Europe, North America, and Australia. It's a newer custom in other countries. In 1958, it was introduced to Japan by an enterprising candy company and now there is a gender battle amidst Japanese graciousness. February 14 is a one-sided event in Japan with women giving giri-choc, which translates literally to *obligation chocolates*. As it has evolved women give gifts of chocolate to men they are grateful to such as bosses, co-workers, brothers, fathers, and friends. Husbands and boyfriends are given honmei-choco (prospective winner chocolates). Nearly half of all chocolate sold in Japan is around February 14.

On March 14, the Japanese men have their turn to reciprocate with White Day, but they are giving marshmallow candy (cheaper in value) and white chocolate and not all women are remembered. These women, mostly young professionals, don't like that and every year they complain about the inequity of giving expensive chocolate against the possibly of receiving marshmallow candy.

Korea does the same Valentine's Day-White Day combination as in Japan and in China they celebrate something like Valentines on the seventh day of the seventh lunar month (known appropriately as the Night of Sevens). Young girls traditionally demonstrate their domestic arts, especially melon carving, on this day and make wishes for a good husband.

In Thailand, Valentine's Day is new, but welcomed as it gives the loving Thais something new to smile about when they can find another reason to dine out and exchange gifts. If you happen to be a single woman visiting England on Valentine's Day it may be beneficial to know that romance is going to the birds. Superstition has it that if the first bird you see is a robin you will marry a sailor, first spying a sparrow you will marry a poor man, and if you see a goldfinch, your husband will be a millionaire.

With so many Romeos and Juliets in February, romantic dinners, music, and movies make a good fare. One of the best remembered romantic songs came from the 1997 movie, *Titanic,* and it was crooned by Celine Dion. *My Heart Will Go On* has made millions of people around the world think about undying love. Although *Titanic* had a romantic theme and is the highest grossing film of all time ($1.8 billion), I remember *Somewhere in Time* with Jane Seymour and Christopher Reeve as being more elegant in sentiment, but less profitable. It was filmed in 1980 at the Grand Hotel on Michigan's Mackinac Island.

All of us are the products of men and women who loved one another. It is our human heritage from parents, grandparents, and more distant ancestors who came together in a spirit of romance that have given us our own lucky chance to freshen that spirit.

Years ago, I remember my grandmother, Murl Mae Welch, who was in her mid-90s at the time, tell me that not a day passed in which she didn't miss my grandfather. He'd been dead for 25 years. That simple statement from a woman in love taught me the best spirit of devotion that many of you already aspire to. Cards, chocolates, flowers, and the other symbols of love on Valentine's Day are nice, but there is no substitute for the good relationships we are nurturing day-in and day-out.

Caregivers and Mentors

Arriving in the world as nothing more than a helpless tiny soul, we are totally dependent on those around us. We squirm, cry, coo, laugh, and spend inordinate amounts of time staring at things. As we get older that dependency becomes less obvious as we strive to stand on our own two feet, feel grown up, and act with independence. But we never outgrow our dependency on those around us. We are always needy for humanity, it is the connection to encouragement, love, and recognition that makes us whole and determines our success and survival.

No one can predict the outcome of a life, but it is certain we couldn't navigate the paths we find ourselves traveling without the caregivers and mentors who are there with encouragement. If you're like me and everyone else there have been a lifetime of snap, crackle, and pop personalities, all of them a standout in charisma. None were ordinary; all extended themselves for others, mostly giving encouragement and ideas to grow character. If any of us fit the definition of a "class act" it is because there has been a corps of good people who instilled balance and then helped us maintain it through a healthy respect for humanity. Lessons in life from these angel-like people ultimately allow us to earn the respect of others.

When you think about your life you'll realize how many family members, friends, neighbors, teachers, colleagues, and bosses contributed to your assimilation of our most important lessons.

Start with our parents and grandparents who teach the basics of discipline. Those lessons didn't easily take to me well because of my personality. Psychology books on child development say that we have a bursting of brain power that doubles our knowledge every day from birth to age four. Think about how profound that is and how important it is to learn the right lessons.

During those years, from the time my two little legs could steadily move me through fields and across streams; I was exploring my small world while parents made efforts to control my wanderlust. My mastery of stubbornness (or is that persistence?) from an early age was classic. On a more positive note, I learned about never telling a lie and being a kind, polite kid. From my depression-era grandparents I learned frugality, one grandmother had made a science of how many sheets of toilet paper a child should use in wiping their butt (it was never enough).

Social scientists say that half of what we grow to be is genetically driven. The other half is our environment, i.e., experiences with people and books are paramount in importance. Educationally, I started out well enough under Mary Farrar, my teacher at a one-room schoolhouse in Michigan. Mrs. Farrar was my guiding light from first grade through the fifth. She liked me, gave me confidence through her encouragement, and also top grades. I don't know if I merited her high opinion because within a few years I was wasting an embarrassing amount of time in secondary school. My grades were miserable; I had poor concentration, and was on the road to nowhere.

During high school years I had two outstanding achievements. One was delivery of the *Detroit Free Press* under route manager Elmer Trimm. Elmer promoted discipline and reliability. He had a way of letting you know if you disappointed him and that made you feel like a worm.

My other mentor was the Reverend Leroy Cabbage, pastor at the People's Presbyterian Church. As a teenager, I was the church janitor and if not a star, at least a weekly participant in Reverend Cabbage's youth leadership meetings. Mrs. Farrar, Mr. Trimm and Reverend Cabbage were authentic youth mentors and an inspiration in their devotion to personal betterment and integrity. We're lucky to have had people like them in our lives. You can't teach good judgment, which comes from having someone instill confidence, compassion, a sense of fair-mindedness, and an understanding of human nature. Helping kids become better in all these areas is one of life's highest callings, whether teacher, preacher, or a youth employer.

Narrowly completing requirements for high school graduation, I shipped out for service with the U.S. Navy.

My original Navy mentor was George Miller, a boot camp company commander at San Diego, California. Miller was a cigar-chomping World War II veteran, master seaman, and a gruff, no nonsense ass-kicker. He took pride in having the best whale boat racing teams in recruit training. For reasons of bad luck and an unfortunate gathering of human chemistry, our team was consistently last at the finish line and that didn't make life any easier. As Miller's cronies ribbed him unmercifully about his losing team, he became energized to transform losers to winners. Even though we weren't much as oarsman on a whale boat, the teenagers in my company came to respect Miller. We also learned respect for one another as well as ourselves. In Miller we found the qualities of a course, but effective teacher, big brother, and friend. Although we continued to be underpowered oarsmen, thanks to his unrelenting enthusiasm, a myriad of wayward boys got started on becoming decent young men.

Over the course of 24-years service others gave me a boost: In 1964, I was a young U.S. sailor working in Washington, DC, when Commander Dale Ward used his visionary talents to predict I would have a highly successful Navy career. Coming from him that was a high compliment. He was a 30-year veteran with a limited formal education who had worked himself up the ranks by sheer street smarts. His rough exterior was intimidating, but with a wife and eight children there was also a tender, kind spot that he showed in mentoring young people.

I didn't share his confidence in my future, but that's the way we tend to be. When young, we hear these comments but simply don't have the experience to trust seasoned wisdom. Because he took the time to express his faith in me, my confidence as a Navy professional grew. Now, thanks to Commander Ward's example when I see light in others I let them know they're on the right track.

Later I became a member of Toastmasters International, a global educational movement to help people become better speakers, listeners, thinkers, and leaders. In 1995, after a few years of giving it my best, I met the President of Toastmasters International, Pauline Shirley, who shared her enthusiasm, wherewithal, and devotion to people. Her example and willingness to focus encouragement on me gave me the confidence to extend myself. Although my influence has always been minuscule compared to her prestige and scope, I've diligently applied myself to helping people better understand their human potential. Without her influence where would I be in that regard?

Another friend and mentor was Jim O'Hara, whom I met while working and living in Puerto Rico. Jim was a U.S. government bureaucrat on an inspection tour of my Navy base. It was a lucky meeting and the start of a lifelong friendship. Jim ultimately became my boss when I retired to Federal civil service. He not only mentored and shared his values on being a professional employee, but also encouraged me as a scholar and long distance runner. My tendency is toward being pudgy and he also badgered me to stay fit and trim. Although Jim retired in 1995, he continues to be a refreshing wellspring of wisdom, humor, and encouragement (but I am still pudgy).

There have been thousands of incredible people who have helped me through life, so many I can't remember all the names. There were high school classmates, my shipmates in the Navy, Toastmaster friends, breast cancer survivors, homeless people, sick and orphaned children, elderly shut-ins, civil service colleagues, my fellow runners, and a myriad of fabulous foreigners from all walks of life. We're all pilgrims on a marvelous journey; the people we meet are what makes the trip enjoyable. There are no days in our lives when someone doesn't bring us something beneficial, generally delivered in person. It might be a good word, a smile, a handshake or a sincere compliment - and there are no days in which we don't extend ourselves in a like manner. That's our blessing as human beings. The only way we can make it better is by giving more kindness and love; you know the people who need it most.

Students of Global Learning

Several weeks ago I had the fortunate experience of visiting with students at Singapore's Insead Business School. Insead is one of the foremost and largest graduate schools for the award of advanced degrees in international business. With a main campus at Fontainebleau, France, and a secondary school in Singapore, Insead also has an alliance with USA's Wharton School. Motivated students from everywhere are at Insead diligently working toward Master's and Doctorate degrees in international business.

Memory fails me to recall whether I was invited or volunteered to give a talk promoting Toastmasters International. My shared view of Toastmasters is that it is a strong complimentary educational experience to studies in business. During the lunchtime program I was inspired to be part of the high mental energy that characterizes groups of ambitious people. I met students from France, Germany, India, Singapore, Spain, U.S.A., and the U.K.

My talk focused on development of self-confidence, self-esteem, and improvement of humanitarian values to accompany the global successes that these students will experience in their future. I could have drawn on any of hundreds of people who have brought history alive with the flowering of their humanity, but the personality I chose to best illustrate educational excellence, unwavering commitment, and strong humanitarian values was the brilliant German medical missionary, Dr. Albert Schweitzer (1875-1965).

Dr. Schweitzer was one of the smartest cookies in our human family earning four Ph.Ds before age 38. He had become a prominent musicologist (one of Europe's foremost organists and an expert on Johann Sebastian Bach), theologist (a popular Lutheran minister who preached at St. Nicholas Church at Strasbourg, Germany), philosopher (innovative thinker and writer on his concept, Reverence for Life), and a medical doctor.

At 21, Dr. Schweitzer, resolved to study until he was 30 and then dedicate his life to a direct service to mankind. In 1905, he made the decision to serve the medically underserved people in Gabon, Africa. Dr. Schweitzer later wrote about his decision, *I wanted to become a doctor in order to be able to work without words....For years I had used theory. My new occupation would be not to talk about the gospel of love, but to put it into practice.*

He entered medical school, completing his last Ph.D and medical internship in seven years. While studying in medicine he continued to give organ concerts and write about theology and philosophy. Of note, when he told family and friends of his decision to devote himself to medicine and the care of African natives, the reaction was mixed. Some wept because they thought that they were losing him, others were angry because to them he was squandering his considerable talent in a far off place that would offer small recognition or reward. The good doctor calmly soldiered on!

After arrival at Gabon, he established a modest facility that specialized in the treatment of malaria, leprosy, elephantiasis, dysentery, and sleeping sickness. In his first year he treated 2,000 people. Schweitzer returned to Europe fourteen times between 1913 and his death in 1965. On these trips he raised funds for his hospital by performing in organ concerts and speaking to civic groups. Further, he recruited doctors, nurses, and other staff members as the hospital expanded. In 1940, The Albert Schweitzer Fellowship was founded in the U.S.A. to support his medical work in Africa. Today Gabon's Schweitzer Hospital serves 35,000 outpatients and 6,000 hospitalizations annually and the staff is an impressive assembly of expatriate medical professionals.

Remarkably, throughout his life he continued to write about theology, music, and philosophy. In all, he published 21 books. His life was also the source of hundreds of books and articles;

he was honored with degrees, citations, scrolls, and the everyday postage stamp. In 1951, he authorized the Animal Welfare Institute to strike a medal in his honor to be presented annually for outstanding achievement in animal welfare. In 1957, he starred in a documentary of his life that was awarded an Oscar by the Academy of Motion Picture Arts and Sciences as the year's best documentary. His life was filled with honors that he modestly accepted, however, the crowning achievement was a 1952 Nobel Peace Prize.

In his presentation speech for the Nobel Peace Prize, Gunnar Jahn, Chairman of the Nobel Committee, said, *...Albert Schweitzer will never belong to any one nation. His whole life and all of his work are a message addressed to all men regardless of nationality or race.*

The contribution that Dr. Schweitzer made was less as a jungle pioneer or saint, than by setting a lifelong example of humanity that has changed the lives of millions that he never met. In a world suffering from a lack of luminaries like Dr. Schweitzer, Mahatma Gandhi, and Martin Luther King, it may be more essential than ever that we follow Dr. Schweitzer's legacy to respect people more, try to understand each other better, and extend kindness more often than we do.

Knowing about Albert Schweitzer's inspiring life is a complement to anyone's education, but none more so than students who are learning about commerce in the international community. Once you know about Dr. Schweitzer it's not easy to forget and where there is a memory there is a hope that we can incorporate some of his faith and love for humanity into our own behavior. I believe that's what the Insead students will do!

Misunderstanding

If there was a planet called Misunderstanding most of us could easily qualify for a visa, and once there, we'd find comfort in seeing so many of our friends and relatives as residents. We humans are amazingly good at innocently producing anxieties and tension through misunderstandings. It starts on the playground, maybe at the teeter-totter where we impulsively think dumping someone makes for a good time.

On Misunderstanding, people are walking around angry and distrustful of one another. Spouses are on edge because they suspect their counterpart doesn't get it. Teenagers are angrily telling their parents: *You don't understand me.* Parents have a similar thought about their kids, they may also feel disappointed that their teenagers can't continue being the charming kids they were when they were cute five and six year olds; customers are leery of sales people because, well, they just don't trust them.

Democracy is weak on Misunderstanding, the problem is that the citizens don't trust politicians and the politicians have an impression that people don't care. The bosses there don't have empathy; morale and productivity are low as employees spend more time grumbling about disconnected communications than creating much of anything positive. Patients cringe with anxiety at the thought of visiting their doctors. They all believe that the docs don't take time to explain their medical situations; doctors are concerned because patients don't follow medical advice.

There are a lot of lawyers on Misunderstanding. They are smart men and women who promote the letter of the law, sometimes unfairly hurting people. There are situations where innocent people are believed guilty until proven innocent. On other days the guilty are found innocent. As the lawyers see it, that's okay, but the people don't understand. Frankly, I don't either.

On Misunderstanding, the populace tends to shout at each other, they feel more confident that their message is being received when the volume is turned up. That's too bad, ensuring that the message is received isn't about volume, it has to do with effective listening. If the people on Misunderstanding knew that being heard isn't about shouting they would all want to take a 5-minute tutorial in good listening practices to improve their situation. The silver lining at Misunderstanding's sad state of human relations is that effective listening is a learned trait, we aren't necessarily born to be good listeners, but we can learn. The reason you should want to listen is basic. Unless you're a little wacko, you want to have good relationships in your life. If you don't realize it, please allow me to be the first to let you know that the quality of your life is dependent upon the quality of your relationships. If you're miserable, uncertain of yourself, feel anxieties, lack confidence, possess poor self-esteem, and the future looks bleak, it's a given that you're not getting along with people very well. Want to change that? Start listening; you will experience a remarkable change. That is a guarantee. Given that you want to get along well with your current and future friends and family members, I can't think of any good reasons why you wouldn't want to listen closely.

The miracle of being an excellent listener, and by default an excellent learner, isn't such a miracle and there are no secrets. Researchers and educators know that when you practice a few basic techniques barriers to good listening breakdown. The first concept is adopting a positive attitude. That shouldn't be a surprise. For my part, I am convinced that people are brilliant and that everyone; including strangers I meet know things that would benefit me. If I am to learn from others, I must be willing to open my mind, close my mouth, and listen. The opposing view is represented by residents on the planet of Misunderstanding; these aliens among us are don't-tell-me-I'll-tell-you types who promote self-centered arrogance. Met any of them lately?

It's easy to identify aliens from Misunderstanding who reside in our midst. They don't let us finish sentences, don't make eye contact, and take opposing views before hearing us out. You can almost see physical barriers hold them back from all they could be. The paradox is that those who have smug attitudes of superiority are anything but superior. They don't know what they don't know, and have relationship problems that will simply get worse as more people become jaded from their negativity. As smugness transforms itself to loneliness, these deaf mutes, crippled by their own poor attitudes, will blame others for their failures. If you have the slightest inking that this profile could be you, run, don't' walk, toward adapting an attitude that will open you up to the blessing of your fellow beings. Start the practice of effective listening.

Experiencing the extraordinary pleasure of listening vs. just hearing what others are saying is a revelation. I'd compare it to the several people I've known who put off getting glasses because they thought it would ruin their good looks. I remember meeting them soon after they received their new glasses and they were in wonderment as they explained how happy it was to see without blurred vision.

As an example, I remember my former neighbor in Herndon, Virginia. As a third grader, Shannon McManus found herself in a personal crisis. Because we love our kids so much we don't like seeing them in crisis, but just like adults they suffer, find solutions and grow. Gifted with a perky personality and very bright, Shannon's grades were sliding, she wasn't on-the-ball in class and her teacher's view was that Shannon just wasn't getting it. The teacher, Shannon, and her mother Betsy compared notes, their initial diagnosis proved correct, the problem was vision. An optometrist confirmed that Shannon could only see effectively for about four feet. The blackboard and the rest of the world was a blur. Adorned with her new glasses, Shannon's face showed the expression of someone who had received one of life's greatest treasures, the gift of sight.

Listening, another important sense, also gives us an ability to better visualize when we focus our mind on speakers and their message. In the past decade, I was exceedingly fortunate to be associated with the non-for-profit educational organization, Toastmasters International. First as a student, later as a group leader, I became deeply involved with people and the nuances of public speaking, effective listening, critical thinking (attitude), and leadership. In presenting 58 workshops, the nearly 1,000 participants I facilitated were enthralled with learning how to become a more effective listener. Those in the workshops were universally starved for improved communications with spouses, parents, kids, friends, and supervisions. They were hungry for ideas that would improve relationships.

It was a revelation for us all. I learned how significant poor listening was in the lives of others; the workshop participants developed sensitivity to the importance of listening effectively. Together we practiced ideas that would reconnect them to improved relationships through listening.

If you would like to avoid problems they're having on Misunderstanding: as hard as it may be - keep your mouth shut, don't interrupt; maintain an open mind; and don't prejudge other people's ideas before thinking them through. You'll astonish yourself and those around you with the new enlightened you.

Adventures in Reading

My guess is that there are millions of little blue or pink baby books with the simple entry *...loves reading, especially books with animals...* I was a year old when my mother made that entry in my baby book. Although I wasn't truly reading, I apparently had shown a notable passion for books. How I got my start with reading is lost to posterity. Typically, parents and grandparents read us stories stimulating childhood interest, we learn to turn pages, and then when the book is left within reach, we're off and running to a lifetime of word and picture adventures.

My reading grew to include just about anything with a printed word. While a teenager, I promoted the *Detroit Free Press* as a morning delivery boy. My route manager in Milan, Michigan, Elmer Trimm told me that newspapers were one of the world's best bargains: *For 10 cents a person could be entertained for hours with interesting news from around the world.* I passed this spirit to prospective customers.

Young boys across Michigan were up early everyday spreading the news with their paper routes. Getting up at 4 a.m., I'd ride my bike to the route manager's home, fold 50-60 newspapers in his basement and make deliveries before school started. The reliability of getting the *Free Press* to customer's homes was akin to delivery of the U.S. mail. There were no missed days for bitter cold, deep snow, or heavy rains.

Besides the *Free Press*, my early readings included explorations through my grandparents' back issues of *National Geographic, Look, Reader's Digest,* and other magazines that were heavy on pictures. It was a revelation to see elephants, soldiers and sailors, girls in bathing suits, shiny new cars, airplanes, Eskimos, and movie stars living their lives. There was also the natural wonder of oceans, mountains, and jungles along with the mysteries of the stars.

The magazines my grandparents subscribed to reflected their interests. There were magazines on gardening, fishing, hunting, and farming. The pages told stories about the one that got away or how to enrich soils through better use of manure spreaders. The people on these pages were mostly happy about their successes at bow hunting, fly fishing, or reaping record bushels of wheat. They showed off their new guns, fishing tackle, tractors, and combines.

Reading about Dick and Jane in my early school primers was fine, but the free flow of information about the world was better. It still is, not just for kids, but for people of all ages. From cradle to grave, books, magazines, newspapers, and now the Internet bring us the information we need to stay current with the world. Eventually, our reading abilities start separating us from the pack. Some fall horribly behind in reading comprehension and word knowledge, their vision and self-confidence are affected, they get stuck wherever they happen to be at the time. There are people in America who are 50 years old but still in the fourth grade, they just scrape by, that's sad, and so unnecessary.

My early theory on adult learning, or the lack of it, was that when people don't make the effort to learn new information about the world they regress. In short, if we do nothing to expand our minds, our knowledge of the world shrinks. Now, it's my belief that we're not really getting mentally trimmer from our information diet, it's just that many of those around us are progressing forward in their mental fitness so much faster. They make us look like we're standing still. Picture two runners at the start line, the whistle blows to signal the beginning of their race. One runner sprints forward, the other stands still. Which of the two runners will happily win the race?

Balancing yourself in a world where man's knowledge doubles every few years requires a disciplined effort to keep current. If we don't work to maintain the status quo with a world moving forward, we fall behind to the eventual loss of our relevancy. Our confidence and pride suffer as co-workers, friends, and family count us out. None of us have to evolve into fuddy-duddies. We can feed our minds nourishment by reading and listening, contribute value to those ideas through mental massage, and then pass them along to others. If your thoughts are positive and helpful to others, you've just made the world better. Does that sound cool? I think it is.

If you haven't been exercising your mind by reading, it will take discipline to get started. It's true that life's biggest rewards go to those who work hardest. There aren't any shortcuts to achievement of worthwhile goals. They come to us by our exercise of courage, discipline, sheer devotion, and energy. Are those personal qualities in short supply? One-third of Americans don't pick up another book after high school, forty percent of college graduates quit reading books, and ninety-eight percent of Americans don't own a free library card. What do you think?

The books I like best are about people's lives, economics, politics, travel, spirituality, and historical reference. These volumes are best for me because they teach and inspire, I acquire ideas that raise my standards. Learning how others cope with illness, death, and prosperity; develop their mantras for success; and benefit others with their goodness--lifts me to new heights. I become better connected to humanities past and present, and that improves my prospects for the future.

My friend Ginny Kibler, a Washington, DC-based economist, has a nice way of describing the benefits she receives from reading: *Reading makes life interesting. I enjoy talking about what I read to others and learning from them about what they are reading. So let's say reading makes me a good conversationalist. Reading has helped me in job interviews...my reading expands my knowledge base, opens my mind to ideas, concepts, theories and philosophies that help me analyze issues on my job. I find that I have so much to bring to any issue, many times much more in the way of perspective than others.* Ginny concludes with a powerful statement, *Reading inspires me to be a better person, to continue learning and growing."*

To quote Thomas Jefferson, *I could not live without books.* One of the best benefits of living in a democratic society is the opportunity to learn and grow through reading, research, and the exchange of ideas. When we don't do it our political processes, culture, and economy suffer, all good reasons to be our best through reading.

Farewell Bobbie

Last week, my former girlfriend, ex-wife, and good friend, Roberta "Bobbie" Culp passed away after years of bravery and courage in a valiant struggle with cancer. I mention Bobbie because in the many years that I knew her she was a class act in striving to be her best, encouraged others to be the same, and was a perennial inspiration.

She trusted God and her own intuition, was a trophy mother, loving and supportive daughter, and instantly liked by everyone who crossed her path. Her smile and infectious laughter attracted people who immensely enjoyed her company.

Bobbie marched to her own drum beat starting with U.S. Navy enlistment in 1960 to get training as a dental technician, but wound up as a cryptologist in Washington, D.C., instead. She chose military service before it was in fashion, the number of women admitted was small and their career opportunities limited. Following her three year enlistment we were married and throughout our marriage she lived in Maryland, Michigan, Spain, Texas, and Oklahoma.

Ambitious to the core, she made good choices in education ultimately completing a master's degree to qualify as a Family Nurse Practitioner. Her main calling was as a health care provider at the Flathead Indian Reservation in Western Montana.

Besides her admirable personal qualities one of the things that impressed me most was her enthused willingness to involve herself in new and challenging endeavors. A good example of this was while we were living in Spain she was offered the opportunity to host a weekly radio show on Armed Forces Radio. Given that she tended toward the shy side, like most of us, she should have politely declined with one excuse or another. Instead, she accepted the offer, pushed forward, learned about radio broadcasting, and her show was a huge success. Loaded down with two toddlers, preparing for her radio show, and maintaining a home in a Spanish neighborhood wasn't enough for Bobbie. When the opportunity arose to sell Tupperware in the community she again overcame her reluctance, learned to speak Spanish and became a wonderful American ambassador to the many Spanish women she met.

Following our divorce, Bobbie took the high road to adventure along with two small children to Alaska, where she tried to settle into a new life. But adjustment to the high cost-of-living from the lower 48-states forced a retreat to Montana, her home state. It was there that her life changed in meeting and marrying, Dr. Steve Culp, a dentist who had recently given up his practice in Indiana for a new life on one of America's final frontiers.

Her most difficult and persistent challenges in life came through combating cancer. In 1982, she was diagnosed with breast cancer that had metastasized (spread) to her lymph nodes. Following surgery for a double mastectomy, she awoke in her room to a bright light and loud voice that said, *your body is cancer free!*

The following morning her doctors visited to discuss chemo therapy, which she refused. Although Bobbie was a medical professional, the doctors reminded her that she'd be dead within a year without the therapy. When pressed, she explained that her body was cancer free. Frustrated, the doctors agreed to retest her lymph nodes. To their disbelief she was, indeed, cancer free.

Following this life changing experience she did just that, changed her life. She worked less and devoted herself more to fitness and the outdoors that she loved by skiing, hiking, camping, fishing, cave climbing, bow hunting, and gardening. In 1997, she won a gold medal as a race walker in the Montana Senior Olympics. Bobbie was multitalented and had many interests. She loved art and music, was an avid reader and writer, and artist creating beautiful stained glass art.

One of her proudest career achievements was helping to establish a nursing curriculum at the Flathead Indian Reservation's Salish Kootenai College.

Her finale started about six years ago when the cancer metastasized to a vertebra on her spine. Advised that the bone must be removed and the surgery would put her at risk of being paralyzed, she took a chance given that there wasn't a good alternative. Following the operation she was paralyzed from the waist down. Doctors advised that she'd never walk again. In one of her finest moments she confidently said she thought they were wrong and that she would walk. Through Spartan heroics in physical therapy, nine months later she was on her feet and taking unaided steps forward.

As bad luck would have it, the cancer spread again to other bones, then the brain, liver and lungs. The medications were a drain, but she never lost her balance in expressing firm optimism about the future.

Bobbie was the daughter of a pioneering family, the Zimmermans. She was tough, compassionate, and inspiring as a mother, wife, health care professional, teacher, and friend. She passed away peacefully at her country home in Charlo, Montana, with daughter Christina Rae, son Bill, sister Penny, and a host of loving relatives. In the shadows were Joe and Salie, her cat and dog.

Farewell Rosemary

Rosemary Williams, 60, of Silver Spring, Maryland died June 4 in her home after a year-long fight with cancer. She was Director of Howard University's Cancer Center Tumor Registry. She is survived by her children Anthony C. Williams, Jr., Ashburn, Virginia; and Sabrina L. Williams of Germantown, Maryland; and four grandchildren.

Around the world there are over 150,000 deaths every day, people are dying from all sorts of unfortunate causes...there simply isn't a good cause of death. Most of these people don't have obituaries and some are buried in small family plots with little fanfare. We deserve better. When we lose a fabulous human being from our midst, I suppose the truth is words simply can't convey the sense of lose and all the meaning that one life has on another.

Rosemary Williams was a long distance friend and former colleague in the struggle to overcome breast cancer. I never met a more kind or thoughtful woman. For 10 years we worked together in Washington to raise money for breast cancer research and treatment; and create awareness for the importance of early detection of breast cancer. Well respected in her community, Rosemary was a powerful influence on others to do better in their lives.

After I relocated to Singapore in 2002, she wrote frequent e-mails about her continuing efforts to combat cancer along with encouragement that ideas in *On the run...* were striking a responsive chord. Several months before she died, Rosemary sent me the following story she had written about her brother Conrad. I've read it several times and with each reading feel her sister-love and marvel at her brother Conrad's life of adventure and service to others. I am reprinting it as a tribute to Rosemary and her brother, and to help us all think about doing better in our lives.

The Greatest Danger of All

"You know the things we fear most are not the things that happen. Often times the dangers come from the things that we do not fear, because those are the ones that we are not keeping alert to prevent from happening.

"My handsome brother, Conrad, was the first born of my parents' three children. He was born May 6, 1942, in Homestead, Pennsylvania, and except for one year in the Washington, DC area while he was on WOL Radio (as music director and newscaster from 1969-1970), he spent his life in Pittsburgh, Pennsylvania. He also spent three years in the U.S. Army from 1960 to 1963.

"When Conrad was a baby a fortune teller, who was knocking on doors in the neighborhood, told my mother he would break many a heart as a man. That was an understatement. A lot of teenage girls wanted to be my friend in high school, so that they could come to Conrad's house. At first I thought I was just extra well liked, until one young lady confessed she was really coming by my house so often to get a glimpse of my brother. Even though he married only once, he had so many girlfriends (many at the same time) that I cannot begin to remember all their names.

"At about age 11 or 12, Conrad decided he wanted to box in the Golden Gloves. My parents were terrified. They knew one young man personally who had a permanent brain injury from boxing. My brother had a mind of his own and boxed for a number of years as an amateur and had a few professional fights in his early 20's. He lost only one fight which was a decision. My father believed he would have done well as a welterweight boxer, but lost 3 years from the sport when he joined the military at age 18.

"Another danger came as one ended! My brother joined the US Army's 82nd Airborne. Of all things, he was jumping out of airplanes! My mother and I prayed daily for this paratrooper. Years later, my brother shared with me that he could not believe he was jumping out of planes. He had to be young to have done that. He went through a number of years when he would not fly in a commercial jet, because he was afraid of planes after an incident over the Gulf of Mexico. He and other soldiers were returning to Fort Bragg from Panama when one of the plane's engines went out. My brother was at the door ready to parachute out, but the other guys stopped him and they all made it back to Fort Bragg on one engine.

"He married and had a family after military service. My family and I were breathing fine when he decided to become a disc jockey, later newscaster and talk show host on the radio. He was so admired by former teachers and classmates that he became something of a Pittsburgh celebrity. Then at age 33 he decided to fulfill his lifelong dream of becoming a law enforcement officer. He was a uniformed Pennsylvania State Police Officer for a number of years and then became an undercover officer. Much to the horror of my family, he spent about 25 years in this job. He was to retire in 2002 due to the required age 60 retirement for the Pennsylvania State Police. Then...

"He said to me one day that he felt something in his chest near his sternum. I told him to immediately see his doctor. He did not at that point, but did see the doctor several months later. A CT Scan of the chest was done. It showed a right lung mass. Being in the cancer field, I was horrified. He had been a cigarette smoker for 44 years. He had escaped so many dangers in life; I just believed that he would come out of this also.

"Conrad was admitted to a hospital for biopsy. He had his surgeon phone me to tell me the news since my field was cancer and he wanted me to make any decisions about his care. He had "squamous cell carcinoma" of the lung. There was no doubt that this type of cancer is cigarette related.

"Someone who had survived boxing, parachuting, and bullets as a state trooper now couldn't escape lung cancer. The greatest danger of all was his cigarettes. I had tried to tell him for years to stop smoking, but he just laughed off my fears.

"The American Cancer Society estimated that in 2005 there were more than 175,000 cancer deaths caused by tobacco use. When Conrad began smoking at age 16, death at age 59 ½ was hard for him to imagine.

"I want all the beautiful young people who smoke to know that life is very short, so please do not rush it away. Quit now while you have a chance to change the course of your life. Look for smoking cessation programs or just realize you need to quit for your loved ones who would be devastated by an untimely loss caused by what may also be your greatest danger of all."

Farewell Uncle Noun

Living in Thailand gives ample reminder of how the fabrics of our lives are woven from the same thread, but the pattern may be slightly different. Forty years ago, I heard an Asian expression that may state this sentiment best, *Samo, samo, only different.*

The hero of this story is Uncle Noun Bootiem, 76, rice miller, devout Buddhist, and patriarch of his family. Physically strong from a lifetime of hoisting 50 kg (110 pound) bags of rice, he continued to ride his bicycle or motorbike to work every day.

Four weeks ago, Uncle Noun (pronounced noon) rose from his bed, felt faint, and fell to the floor with a stroke. He couldn't get up because of paralysis on his right side and he'd lost his speech. Let's follow his experiences with his first major illness, family conflict, his first-ever hospitalization, love of a devoted family, more conflict, and finally his cremation in a patch of jungle not far from his wooden home on stilts.

Living in the small farming village of Ban Pungkae in the Mekong River Valley, word travels fast about friends and relatives. Within minutes of his collapse his modest home was filling with those people who were most important in his life. As the close-knit family gathered, his sister took center stage asking the group whether they should consult a fortune teller or go to the temple and pray. Smaller voices mentioned doctors, medical tests, and hospitalization. The little voices gathered volume and practicality came to rule. Unfortunately it was a busy time for the ambulance and it was several hours before he was transported to the small hospital at Srisongkram, 11 miles from home. Immediately upon arrival doctors ordered him moved to the provincial hospital at Nakhon Phanom, 36 miles southeast.

This is where I first saw Uncle Noun as I helped lift him from his stretcher to the MRI for a brain scan. The scan revealed hemorrhaging and the old miller was put back into an ambulance for travel to the larger hospital at Sakhon Nakhon, 63 miles away. Twenty relatives trailed behind to lend their support.

Twelve hours after his stroke it was 8 pm and a successful operation was underway to relieve pressure on the brain. He was moved from the operating room to an open-bay intensive care unit with 15 other patients. All the patients were attended to by relatives under supervision of a small nursing staff. In Uncle Noun's family four relatives cared for him in 24-hour shifts, sleeping on mats and eating sticky rice, noodles, vegetables and fruit in a picnic style. Their job was to watch over his condition and turn him over every two hours. At his home in the village, another team of four relatives stayed with Aunt Loang, 80, who is frail, missed her husband, and was a stroke victim herself four years earlier.

Several days later I returned to visit the old man who was now stable, but given only a 20 percent chance of living another day. After my visit I sat beside a grassy courtyard outside of ICU. In looking around I noticed that the windows were open (no air conditioning) and there were no screens in mosquito country. As the days passed Uncle Noun willfully clung to life, but there was a parade of deaths as people around him died from various infections.

Five days after his operation, there was a gathering of 40+ relatives at his home to pray for his recovery. There was also eating and drinking. Lowering my diplomatic guard, I wore retiree togs: jogging shoes, t-shirt, and trekker pants. As you already know, shoes are removed before entering an Asian home. This is a good practice as it helps maintain spotless cleanliness. Removing my shoes, white running socks showed some wear and tear with holes here and there. One of the men mentioned to my business partner, Wanvisa Techo, that it was little wonder I was a rich man because I didn't waste money on socks. The next day I demonstrated a partial reformation by buying new socks, but saved the old ones for special occasions. Why are some men this way?

Several days later Uncle's daughter and son made a difficult decision. They decided it was best to take the old guy off of life-supporting oxygen and transport him home to die. This was an unpopular decision among the majority as there was a consensus that he deserved a month on life-support to regain his strength.

A few hours after returning home, Uncle Noun passed peacefully; by 10 am the following morning, two large tents had been erected outside his home, food was being prepared, and several hundred mourners arrived to extend their respects. After lunch of noodle soup, sticky rice and pork, fried chicken, and vegetables, Thai whiskey and cold beer were passed. With a chance to make up for the sock episode, I drew generously on the rice whiskey as a show of respect for Thai culture and the memory of Uncle Noun. It was a popular effort.

At 3 pm, his coffin with incense, candles, wreathes and a handsome picture of him was placed on the back of a pickup truck. A burst from an M-16 rifle was fired and fireworks exploded. These were to clear his way for a straight shot to heaven. Although the truck moved on its own power, a long white narrow cloth was tied to the truck and pulled by 10 saffron-robed monks. The procession of several hundred people walked behind the truck for a half-mile into a jungle clearing where the coffin was put into a pyre of large logs. The Buddhist monks, always their best at funerals, chanted melodiously as family and friends deposited more candles and incense around the coffin.

The logs were ignited and the smoke containing Uncle Noun's spirit rose, but didn't head straight for heaven. The smoke curled back toward the village of Ban Phu Katae, which is where he had his rice mill. This was interpreted as a restless spirit concerned about his business.

That night a woman who owed him money heard noises outside her home. She investigated and found no one. Later closing her eyes, she saw Uncle Noun's face. She got up, packed her suitcase, and has taken up temporary residence in a new location.

Regardless of your age, nationality, or religion, there are obvious lessons from Uncle Noun's experience. Some that come to mind: live each day at your best, enjoy your family and friends, don't worry so much about the little things, tell your kids not to pull the plug too quickly, and wear presentable socks on formal occasions.

A Road Less Traveled

Two weeks ago I took a Sunday afternoon drive on an out of the way farm-to-market road near my home at Nakhon Phanom. The dirt road was only wide enough for a car and motorbike to pass side-by-side. The route passed through small villages that were aligned along the Mekong River like pretty pearls in a necklace.

It was an interesting journey of bamboo forests, verdant rice paddies, and curious water buffalo grazing beside the road. Water buffalo, like cows, are curious creatures, maybe even suspicious of strangers. They make you feel more important than you are by not taking their eyes off of you. We know that God gave these creatures horns for some good purpose and behind those innocent eyes may be the idea: *If you touch one blade of my grass I will make you sorry!*

There were also farmers bicycling along underneath a blue sky dotted with dark clouds that hinted of a tropical shower. They wore the traditional cone-shaped straw hats that protect wearers from rain and sun all over Southeast Asia. Across the Mekong River were the faraway mountains of Laos with peaks poking up through a hazy gray mist.

The villages along this road contain wooden houses on stilts, which is the traditional building style in Esan (variable spelling Isan, Isaan), my region of Thailand. The raised houses allow a cooling breeze to pass underneath the house and better protect people from flooding. Cooking, eating, socializing, and handicraft work is conducted with neighbors in the cool area beneath the house.

One of the most popular handicrafts is the weaving of multicolored reed mats. The reeds are cut, dried, split, dyed, and then weaved into pretty patterns. The mats are then used by the family for eating, sitting, and sleeping. Walking into a farm home in Esan is an adventure in simplicity. There is little furniture, a gas burner and/or charcoal burner for cooking, aluminum pots, a few wardrobes for clothing, and rolled up mats that are unrolled for sleeping. There are usually no tables or chairs, people sit on mats, sleep on mats, and eat on mats. House interiors are spotlessly clean; no one wears shoes or sandals.

Esan wooden homes aren't usually painted and are surrounded by flocks of chickens, sometimes ducks, geese or turkeys, domestic cattle, and water buffalo. Yards and gardens are blazing with brightly colored tropical flowers and vines, fruit trees (especially banana trees), and coconut trees grow like weeds. There are also small garden plots where herbs, vegetables, and peppers are grown. They are collected for salads that complement rice, noodles, and fruits in the everyday diet.

Hoes, shovels, machetes, carts, small sheds, fish pond, hand-washed clothes hanging on a line, small tractor, one or two motorbikes, bicycles, and a TV antennae round out the farm complex.

The farmers have a fish pond to diversify their livelihood and diet. It is an idea promoted by the King. King Blumibol Adulyadej encourages waterworks of all sorts to allow the Esan people to have stable sources of water from rivers and reservoirs. Although all the water is polluted (except from the deepest wells) and must be boiled before drinking, it is indispensible for irrigating the rich rice crops that farmers depend upon for consumption and sale. Nakhon Phanom gets 132 inches of rainfall annually (the second greatest total in Thailand), but most of Esan is not as abundantly supplied by Mother Nature and there are some long dry spells.

Notwithstanding the famous Siamese cat, Thai people aren't crazy for cats, but love their dogs and most families have two or three. They look healthy, well-fed, and bark at strangers. Some of these four-legged best friends bypass the pretense of friendliness and go right for the growl.

People also stare at foreigners, the reason being they see so few of them. On this trip and on my daily jogs I am treated like a celebrity, sometimes I stop at a farmhouse to give a traditional Thai greeting, Sawasdee (hello) and make other small talk (all I can manage in Thai). Parents bring their shy children forward to meet the farang (foreigner). Younger people wear Western-style clothing: t-shirts with Spiderman, blue jeans, and shorts. There are an abundance of Detroit Tigers and New York Yankee baseball caps. Older people are in traditional cottons and silks with distinctive Thai patterns in practical wrap-arounds (sarongs). Their dress is reminiscent of past days.

Even the smallest village has a wat (Buddhist temple), which is the center of community life. Every morning a little after 6 a.m., the saffron-clothed monks pass through the village collecting donations from residents. Their shoulders are back, head poised and they walk barefoot with purpose in rain, wind, and heat. Sometimes they carry an umbrella. Contributions usually consist of food, which is then consumed by the monks, poor people and the elderly who may need a helping hand.

Thailand is about the size of Texas with 63 million people. The Esan region and the Mekong River Valley are one distinctive part; all are different with panoramic ocean views, forested mountains, and the glamour of big city living in Bangkok (10 million people). Globalization and Thailand's success at integrating into the world economy is changing the character and personality of the country. The sons and daughters of farmers are getting university degrees; they are migrating away from the land to work in foreign countries or the service and industrial complex around Bangkok.

Life is changing everywhere; no community is standing still in time with the good or bad that that may signal for the future. But I don't usually let such thoughts of the modern Thailand interrupt the peace I find in these lovely Sunday afternoon country settings.

The Subbhana Foundation

Cambodia first entered my consciousness one afternoon in 1968 as I watched several Cambodian fast-attack patrol boats move swiftly and menacingly toward my unarmed technical research ship, USS Oxford. The boats circled several times and luckily returned to their base mistakenly identifying us as an unarmed merchant ship.

Seven years later the lives of the Cambodian people would be upturned in the worst possible way. Following a civil war in which the communist-inspired and Chinese-backed Khmer Rouge took control of the country, a deliberate and systematic destruction of the population was initiated. It lasted four years (1975-1979) until Vietnam intervened with military force. During those four years an estimated two million people (25 percent of population) perished through killing fields. There are over 300 major mass graves scattered around the country and as many as 20,000 in total. The United Nations subsequently designated the tragedy genocide, only the 7th such designation in nearly a hundred years.

Before traveling to Cambodia on a working assignment in 2006, I was aware of the compassionate work being done by American expatriates Christine Wagner and Barbara Rinehart to help Cambodian children and had read five books by victims of the genocide: *Children of Cambodia's Killing Fields*, a compilation of stories by Dith Pran; *When Broken Glass Floats* by Chanrithy Him; *First They Killed My Father* and *Lucky Child* by Loung Ung and *The Stones Cry Out* by Molyda Szymusiak.

These books are all memoirs written by men and women who had miraculously lived through the genocide as 5-10 year old slave laborers. They had watched their parents and siblings die of starvation or mass murder by the Khmer Rouge. These books are sad, but compelling and important reading. The better educated we are regarding these kinds of crimes against humanity, the better able we are to defend against such atrocities in the future. History can't be rewritten, what happened--happened, but good people can make a difference in the future.

A year ago, I spent eight days at Phnom Penh, Cambodia's capital; and Sihanoukville, the country's main port. I visited the former Toul Sleng Prison, known as S-21, which was once the Tuol Svay Prey High School. The 5-building campus processed about 17,000 prisoners, only eight are known to have survived. After torture, the prisoners were moved a short distance outside of Phnom Penh to the Choeung Ek extermination center where 20,000 bodies have been recovered in mass graves. One grave contained only mothers and their babies! Targets of the Khmer Rouge were doctors, teachers, lawyers, government employees, community leaders, police, soldiers, and anyone who wore glasses because that was a sign that they read books and had been educated.

During this trip I probably spoke with a dozen or more middle-aged people regarding their experiences. Each had a sad story, some were stoic but others, even though nearly 40 years had passed, got lumps in their throat and watery eyes from the pain that won't go away. This year, for the first time, the surviving members of the Khmer Rouge leadership are being brought to trial on charges of genocide.

It is with these events in mind that Christine Wagner, a registered nurse, and Barbara Rinehart, a school teacher, and other international women started giving their hearts, time, talent, and extra cash to benefit a daycare center at Battambang, Cambodia. They started their work while living in Singapore during 2000-04. Christine subsequently moved with her family to Georgia while Barbara and her family relocated to Texas. To better formalize and improve the efficiency of their efforts, Christine incorporated a nonprofit organization, *Hearts and Hands for Cambodia.*

Their main social service project is to assist The Subbhana Foundation by supporting the day care center at Battambang. Subbhana is a Khmer women's organization whose mission is to improve the quality of life for women and children in Cambodia. The Day Care houses 110 children ages 2-6 during the weekdays. They provide children with meals and education, including personal hygiene and life skills through consistent, stable, and loving support.

Hearts and Hands has provided them with playground equipment, educational materials and instruction, electricity, video equipment, clothing, towels, and fans, as well as digging a ditch for the rainy season to prevent flooding. The newest project is to start a sponsorship program for the children.

Un Samphors is one of the little girls there. Un will be five years old on October 8. Like all Libras, she's a pretty good kid. She has five brothers and sisters, and lives at Bain Village in Battambang Province. Along with 109 other small fry, she and her family benefit from the educational development and nurturing provided by the Subbhana Foundation Day Care Center at Battambang.

Hearts and Hands for Cambodia is a small nonprofit organization and is forced to compete with thousands of other worthy charities. In essence, that means that the Cambodian kids are competing against big organizations. Because of the small voice of *Hearts and Hands* I am pitching in to help create awareness and asking for whatever help (monetary contribution) you're comfortable in making. As Christine wrote in a recent newsletter, *Children are the same everywhere. They want love and attention and they need positive feedback. The Cambodian children especially are hungry for this. The Day Care is a tremendous opportunity for us to change the lives of not only these children but of the villages where they live.*

Giving Thanks

I don't often join clubs or associations, but sometimes the logic of congregating with my own kind is compelling. Last month, I joined the *Naval Cryptologic Veterans Association*, which then sent me a CD with the name and address of the group's 3,000 plus members.

I looked up Richard Wasilewski first, maybe because in 24 years of Navy service he impressed me most. A few days ago, I wrote him at his home in Clinton, Maryland. None of you know Richard and I haven't seen him for 46 years. But then when we're young and impressionable everything endures in memory: good girlfriends, good advice, and good examples from the people we are around. Dick was my first chief petty officer supervisor and presented such a squared-away professionalism I was influenced to make the Navy a career.

The letter was less than a page, simply giving a brief summary of my career with the Navy, the following civilian service with the Naval Criminal Investigative Service, and an acknowledgement of his good influence that wasn't forgotten. It's healthy to express gratitude and it made me feel good to write him.

The *Naval Cryptologic Veterans Association* is comprised of cryptologists who worked with the Naval Security Group Command and its predecessor organizations. The members and those now serving with the Naval Security Group Command are exceedingly bright, conscientious, and self-sacrificing. For the past 75 years their dedicated service has mostly been shrouded behind a veil of discretionary silence. If that description whets your appetite for more information you can learn more at their website: www.ncva.org.

There is another group of men and women that I want to thank for their inspiration. Many of them I don't know, but they belong to the running club, *50 and DC*. The people in this club are so phenomenal with fitness and motivation you can scarcely believe it. The club's name, *50 and DC*, symbolizes that members have either run or are committed to running a marathon in every state plus the District of Columbia. I joined ten years ago after completing the minimum requirement: 20 marathons in 20 different states (since lowered to ten marathons/ten states). To insure that we'll all on the same page: a marathon is 26.2 miles (43 kilometers). Not so many people dream of running this distance let alone actually spending the hundreds of hours training and then entering that kind of grueling event. In my view it takes a confident mind pushing a reluctant body further than normal human endurance.

A few of the members run a marathon every week, they have completed all 50 states several times and as if that wasn't sufficient, they then do the provinces in Canada and then the seven continents, then they run in the high mountain ranges, across deserts, and in the Arctic. They run ultra-marathons, which is 26.2 plus miles, sometimes a hundred miles. If it were possible to run on water they would be dashing across the Pacific and Atlantic.

When I joined there were 200 members, now there are nearly 1,000. With the big job of pushing human endurance you'd think these are some pretty serious folks, the truth is they are good humored, calm, and centered. They are helpful, encouraging, and many of them come as close to being an angel in their kindness as you can get without being heavenly deputized.

In my 29 years of being around long-distance runners I know of the abundant faith, joy, and optimism that contribute to their well being. It is infectious. The further they routinely run, the greater their creative thought and modesty. I never met so many people endowed with their own truth.

With 28 million plus runners in America, many participating in at least one of 15,000 annual races (one mile through ultra-marathons), it is easy to see why the special men and women of *50 and DC* would want to congregate together. We all like to be with people who are like us, it is comforting, like looking in a mirror at a twin brother or sister who is just like we are in word and deed. That's why people in churches, prisons, schools, senior citizen centers, and other institutions are usually pretty happy - they are in proximity to kindred spirits who validate their direction in life.

Interestingly, I haven't run a marathon since 2000, but my $10 fee guarantees a lifetime membership. Although running longer distances hasn't been a part of my routine recently, I am one of the most prolific writers in the club and they are good enough to feature each issue of *On the run...* as part of their website. If you'd like to learn more about this dynamic group of people, visit www.50anddc.org.

The magnificent human condition shows itself best in people like Richard Wasilewski and those in *50 and DC* What these showstoppers have in common is discipline, self-pride, and confidence in their bearing and mission to be their best. None of them set out to be an influential example to others, but that's what it amounts to when the final tally is taken. What will be your score?

Bali and Java

It may not be a fair description to call travel from retirement a vacation, taking a holiday sounds more technically correct. Three weeks ago, I took a holiday to Bali and Java, Indonesia.

By way of background, Indonesia is one of the more fascinating places on the planet. It is the world's largest Muslim nation and is spread across 19,000 islands, give or take one or two. With over 400 volcanoes (90 active), Indonesia is a shaky earthen platform where it's 230 million people speak over 300 different languages. Either man-made or natural disasters are a way-of-life from earthquakes, flooding, mudslides, volcanic eruptions, tsunamis, crashing airlines, sinking ferries, and bird flu. There are also out-of-control forest fires intended to clear jungle for agriculture, but foul the air over several countries in Southeast Asia.

It's an extremely wealthy country from natural resources, but filled with poor people because of corrupt politicians and government officials. The seeds of corruption have always been a part of the human condition, but Indonesia's President Mohamed Suharto (1966-98) planted criminal roots deeper into his country's moral soil than anyone else. In fact, he holds the record for having the stickiest fingers in world history. With a take of $35 billion diverted from the people's welfare to the pocketbooks and purses of his family and friends, Suharto comes in number one as the most crooked head of state ever. When I am in Indonesia and see the deployable state of roads, hospitals, and schools I think of President Suharto and the light-fingered culture that he nurtured.

Indonesia is also a moderate Muslim country that is tolerant and respectful of other religions. Seldom do I meet a Muslim who is not impressed by Jesus and the miracles he performed to inspire Christianity. My impression is that they are better versed in our Christian faith than we are in understanding Mohammad and his teachings.

First on my travel agenda was flying from Nakhon Phanom, Thailand to Bangkok and then to Densapar, Bali, the world renown resort island. Bali is famous for Hinduism, surfing, attracting tourists, several terrorist bombings, natural beauty, and growing three rice crops annually. The people and nature are gorgeous.

Hinduism might seem out of place in a Muslim country, but 400 years ago Indonesia, then known as the Spice Islands, followed Hindu-inspired Buddhism. Bali is an enclave where its first religion has survived 1,500-2,000 years, but not without the influences of aboriginal animism (all living things possessive of a spirit), Malaya ancestor worship, and aspects of Buddhism. Schools start the day with prayer as do government officials at their meetings. Intuition tells me that praying together at school and work is not such a bad idea in promoting respect, patience, and understanding.

Small prayer baskets made from coconut leaves and bearing water, fruit, flowers, and biscuits are used as a focus of Brahman prayer three times a day. Every day the freshly prepared small baskets are placed outside homes and businesses in Bali as a simple offering. Of interest, the Balinese are the only Hindus in the world who continue to worship Brahman style. The practice was lost in India, 1800 years earlier.

The road to Bali is followed by Americans, Asians, Europeans, and most especially Australians. It is a locale filled with temptations and outright sin. My own downfall came with a visit to McDonalds, and then it was Pizza Hut, and Dunkin Donuts. But you can't beat German or Australian restaurants for signaling that you're in deep trouble at the next weigh-in. Once started it is difficult to contain such urges. Big Macs are lightweights compared to Australia's bangers and mash and meat pies. And before the McDonald's clown started clowning around there was Vienna schnitzel, schweinebraten (roast pork), and bread dumplings, those are specialties at Mama's German Restaurant on Legian Street at Kuta Beach. Like most Balinese restaurants dining is in the open air. But more than that, Mamas has red and white checkered tablecloths to give you a homey feel. These thoughts make my heart beat faster.

Staying at Kuta Beach (a suburb of Densapar) I choose the Camplung Mas Hotel. It is located on a quiet side street two blocks from the surf at Kuta Beach. A solidly pleasant 4-star hotel, the clientele is Australian. It is a plus to be in proximity to the robust and pleasant people from down-under. They are friendly, happy-to-lucky, and enjoy life. The poolside bar and cabana displayed several large Australian flags, the TV played rugby and the beer flowed steadily.

The hotel had lush gardens with fragrant frangipani trees and orchids, fish ponds, and ornate Balinese architecture. Frangipani trees, also known as temple trees, are in the same intoxicating fragrance family as lilacs and wisteria. Because of their uplifting fragrance they are planted in abundance at temples in Bali, Thailand, Indochina, and Singapore. For the curious, the cost for this wonderful hotel was just $30 a day, which included a complimentary breakfast. Living in paradise doesn't have to cost a fortune!

A note about Kuta Beach; it is perfect for jogging. The hard-packed sand is several miles long and eases stress on knees, and off-shore breezes, sound of the surf, and pretty sunbathers make jogging almost effortless. Of interest, North Bali has black sand and the south beaches like Kuta, are a dazzling white. About 1.3 million tourists visit Bali annually with Australia and Japan leading the parade of vacationers or in the case of retirees, holidaymakers. These numbers make Bali the number one tourist attraction in Indonesia.

Leaving Kuta Beach by bus for the island of Java I encountered a six-hour bus and ferry ride along picturesque, but narrow, winding mountainous roads. The roads weren't wide enough for two trucks or buses to pass side-by-side, but they did it anyway with less than inches to spare. I wanted to close my eyes, but survival instincts told me I would better escape an accident with eyes open. Holding my breath and hanging on tight worked just as well.

The bus was called a FrigidKing to commemorate the air conditioning that was once in working order. The coastal road gave inspiring panoramas of terraced rice paddies, coconut groves, blue ocean, and creamy white clouds in a mostly clear sky. As we crossed bridges over pretty streams Balinese women were bathing and washing clothes.

On Java, my final destination was the Muslim farming village of Pasinani (population 5,000), in response to a long standing invitation to visit with a family I'd met 18 months earlier. In this regard my accommodations have never been so meager or hospitality as rich as the week I spent with this family.

Living in a 100-year old brick and masonry home, the family consisted of mother Misati Sri Endang, 47, stroke victim and mother to Rina, 23, and Uut, 16. Others in the home were three orphan girls: Twins Desi and Dewi, 11; and their sister Devi, seven. Misati's husband had deserted the family seven years earlier after selling land, car, and the family home. All the girls were happy to have a brother-father figure if even temporarily.

Every morning from the village I jogged past rice paddies on small country roads to the friendly encouragement of farmers who were consistent in giving thumbs up while roosters were still crowing and cows stared. Generally, someone from the family either jogged along or rode a bicycle as if to watch out for me.

It was early to bed and early to rise as these were hard working farm families. The call to first prayers seemed to come at about 4:15 am and was followed through the day by four additional calls over loudspeakers placed around the village. Further, the prayers were also broadcast. Besides early call to prayers, roosters weren't bashful in spreading the news that it was the dawn of a new day.

174

One morning I took a walk beside a stream on the edge of the village, past rice paddies and into a cow pasture where water buffalo were up to their ears in mud (they love that). I saw butterflies, ducks, a Muslim cemetery, cone-hatted women planting rice shoots, and farmers herding cattle. Later in the afternoon, Rina, the only family member who spoke English, was thumbing through my pocketbook on snakes. From the pictures she identified three specimens that frequent the surrounding countryside: cobras, pit vipers, and kraits. All are dangerous, some deadly. It was too late to cancel my morning stroll.

Before leaving the village there was hugs and handshakes with the grown-ups followed by the right hand being brought to the chest, which symbolizes that I will carry you in my heart. The children took my right hand and brought it to their cheek or forehead meaning that they will always remember me.

The week had passed quickly and the return trip on another FrigidKing bus was underway before I knew it. This time I was more comfortable and didn't feel the need to close my eyes, hold my breath or hang on tight, what happens, happens...life goes on.

Riding the bus, I was happy in feeling that my knowledge of the Muslim people and Indonesia had more than doubled in just a few days and I had been a good American diplomat in the company of extraordinarily fine people. What better way to spend a holiday?

A Michigan Christmas

Michigan is my home with ancestry, family, and friends. The cemeteries are filled with generations of my people. Although dad and mom worked in manufacturing, their parents and those before them were farmers. At this time of the year most farmers are happy to stay indoors and rest. That's my idea of having a good winter.

I don't ice skate, fish on the ice, or snowmobile. A few people I know do like to stick their nose outdoors to feel the nip of Mother Nature. I do that on a limited basis to jog. Yesterday while jogging I slipped and fell on an icy country road. I didn't mind much as it was a soft landing on snow. While jogging in Thailand I sometimes trip on my own feet and the landing isn't so gentle; for years I've tripped on cracks in the sidewalk and twice while jogging in the U.S. I've slipped on ice and knocked myself out. Ouch!

Christmas in Michigan presents unique challenges sometimes faced by Christians in other parts of the world. First, there is the problem of fat grams and our delusion that they don't really matter because it's Christmas. I've told myself that for many years and now look at me. They do matter! My suggestion is not to stuff yourself with our bounty in the name of baby Jesus. He and the Great Father are happier for you just to give a prayer of thanks for something good in your life. Second, we extend our credit cards to the sky, then push a little further toward the universe and think its okay because, well, it's Christmas. Commonsense tells us not to spoil people more than they deserve, but because of our good hearts we do it anyway.

In this part of the world there are more environmental problems that focus on reality. For example, it is winter and that means icicles suspended from rooftops because the frigid temperatures won't let them melt, there are cold winds that numb exposed skin, and pretty flakes of fluffy white stuff that accumulates inch upon inch. In late fall and early winter the color of outdoors is black and brown with blue skies that can change quickly to dark gray. That means it's only a matter of time before we'll see freezing rain, ice or snow. The weathermen practice hype at this time of the year. It's their chance to improve ratings, but none can top the *Today* Show's Willard Scott--a true lover of people and weather. Kids make snowmen here that can live a long time. If you've ever wondered where the snowmen come from that appear in cartoon movies, they are from Michigan. I wouldn't be surprised to see a polar bear any day.

Before Frosty the Snowman and Christmas, people in Michigan were native people born as Ottawas, Chippewa, Potawatomi, and Miami. They also liked to stay in their wigwams in the cold winters. Then the French, British, Irish, Poles, Finnish, Lebanese, and Swedish came. The Finnish and Swedish people love shoveling snow and being in the cold. They make great snowplow operators to keep the roads open during blizzards. We're happy that they chose to resettle here. Now there are 10 million people in Michigan, which is the same population as Bangkok, Thailand, and we have more Dutch than in any other state.

Fifteen percent of the people here don't believe God, while eighty-two percent are Christians. We also have the largest Muslim population (300,000) of any US state. In most of our communities church steeples are the highest structure in town. That is comforting. In those churches you see lovely stained glass windows that seem all the more precious at Christmas. Inside those churches is a treasure of positive spirit from the faithful and you can hear hymns like *Silent Night, Joy to the World,* and *Little Town of Bethlehem.* There are children's programs with the kids singing and reciting details of the Christ child's birth. What the small fry lack in talent they more than make up for in faith and, of course, being lovely kids. If you take your eyes off the children and look at their fathers and mothers you'll see the beaming of parental pride.

Homes and businesses are decorated with bright lights celebrating the season, and there are the sounds of popular music which recalls the birth of Jesus, family reunions, good food, Santa Claus, and a white Christmas. We are sentimental at this time of year. I remember my father every day, but the feeling is more intense at Christmas. For 45 years we had a long-distance relationship except for some Christmas holidays when we'd be together. At those times we'd relish our high caloric intake and he'd tell me stories from his early life. Dad was good about remembering early years, asking him what he did yesterday didn't bear as much fruit!

As a pilgrim traveling from a Buddhist nation, Thailand, to the Christian orientation of America, I am caught between a mostly austere lifestyle to one of comparable opulence. Returning from a small village in Thailand to a small town in America, I passed through Bangkok, the capital of Thailand, and Singapore. Both Bangkok and Singapore have significant Christian populations so the trees and lights are out, kids singing *...here comes Santa Claus, here comes Santa Claus...,* and shoppers are overworking their credit cards. There were blue and pink Christmas trees outside shopping malls and billboards and newspaper ads with Santa encouraging everyone to buy that special gift. In Singapore, I was warmed to see The Salvation Army bell ringers working to benefit the needy.

I am living with my sister Linda in the village of Dundee, which is in Southeast Michigan between Detroit and Toledo, Ohio. Linda's refrigerator is packed with things I like, we're both eating a lot so that we can empty those shelves and get back on our diets. It's a big refrigerator; I don't know how long it will take. My stay is scheduled for 6 weeks and my goal is to fit into one airplane seat on the return trip to Thailand.

Like you, I can always be counted on to do the right thing after exploring the alternatives. This Christmas I'll be neither physically trim nor frugal, but I can strive to retain the spirit of

giving, gratitude and graciousness that mark the Christian spirit.
I have faith that you'll try to do the same!

2008

Reflections on America

I am concluding a spectacular visit in Michigan. The generosity and grandeur of my family and friends is extreme. The secret to the excellence of these relationships may be to only visit now and then, and don't stay too long. My Great-aunt Bernice Beeker, now deceased, had a favorite Ben Franklin quote for such occasions: *Dead fish and company start smelling after 3 days.*

Now having lived overseas the past 5 years, I am more fascinated than ever with the social environment in Michigan and the United States. Some of the things that got my attention were the political campaigning, Britney Spears, bulging supermarket shelves and waistlines (there seems to be a correlation), cold weather, and our economic recession.

The political campaigns, which I can also follow on CNN from my home in Thailand, are interesting from several aspects. First is the high quality of candidates: their experience, patriotism, civility, and ambition.

Among this group of Democratic and Republican candidates are a woman and an African-American, the first in their gender and race to compete for the presidential office. Other remarkable candidates are an enterprising business leader, big city mayor, distinguished congressional leaders, a former prisoner of war, and an ordained minister. Between debates, political ads, telephone surveys, poll results, and the spinning of media personalities it is difficult to determine who the best might be and what positions they profess on one thing or another. None of the candidates have a complete answer to all problems, some are populists with simple but unworkable solutions to complex problems, and others are vague on detailed solutions; however, all are hardworking, on their best behavior, and confident that their leadership is right for the country.

Because America is a democracy it is imperative that good people voluntarily step into the fray to share their visions while exposing their flaws to the scrutiny of our free press. I couldn't do what they do and don't think it's fair to cast stones among them. The media agonizes over nuances, skipping more substantial fare. They do that because it titillates most Americans and that crowds out the important issues that we have with health insurance, immigration, poverty, housing, global warming, government deficit spending, education, gun control, war in Iraq, and economic recession. Hot button issues in America's future must also compete with Britney Spears.

Britney is the tragic heroine of childhood stardom who has seemingly done her best to cope with unique adoration from an early age. Like you and me, she's fragile, but unlike most of us she is in the process of losing all the good that her life has come to represent: marriage, motherhood, family orientation, career success, respect, and personal dignity. She's more popular in the media now than ever before because we in the audience take a perverse interest in tragedy. Not so many people with Britney's status take such a deep plunge and we're bound and determined to drown ourselves in the news. That crowds out prominent events that the free press should be conveying.

Because of a dynamic that promotes trivial pursuit, the media is guilty of not paying enough attention to substance. As an example, think of the hype that created a gung-ho American

181

spirit for the Iraqi War. As the Bush Administration set the tone for hostilities, the media didn't make serious inquiry into allegations against the Iraqi regime; as a result the Administration's misinformation was validated by media indifference. Democracy is weakened when the media, known as the Fourth Estate, mashes down its investigative capacity by focusing on small potatoes.

Supermarket shelves don't bulge with 50 varieties of potato chips and as many kinds of ice cream for no reason. There's money in it as people waddle up and down the aisles filling their carts with the latest fat-gram gimmick. We lead the world in gluttony and the sale of diet books. I don't know where this inordinate desire to consume more than we need started, but it is spreading around the world much to the chagrin of health care providers. We are literally eating ourselves to death. It's neither a happy sight nor happy prospect.

A few days ago, the wind chill was -15F (-26C). I think that's cold and resisted jogging. My friends tell me, *you were born and raised here, you know what it's like. It can't be that bad.* Dear friends, yes, it can. Jogging in this weather gets attention. I am not sure whether it's admiration or shame that someone in the human family could be so faulty in their thinking. Recently, an old farmer pulled up beside me on a country road. His car tires crunched on the snow and ice. Rolling down his window, he offered me a lift. I laughed and told him, *No thanks, I'm purposely doing this for exercise.* He smiled in return saying, *it sure is cold.* I sensed by the look in his eyes he didn't have a lot of confidence in my thought process. Cold weather makes it too easy to avoid physical work, aiding our natural laziness, at least it seems that way in my case.

Michigan is America's recession leader with an unemployment rate of 7.6 percent and 78,000 jobs lost in 2007. We are losing population as people migrate to more prosperous states, our school enrollments and the tax base is sinking, and the housing market is down 34 percent in two years to be one of the worst in the nation. The decay to our prosperity is spreading to Ohio, California, Florida, and other states where economic indicators are weakening. Sadly, our most treasured personal possessions are diminished: faith, hope, and optimism. Politicians in Washington say that the basic fundamentals of our economy are strong while people in Michigan wonder which spaceship they arrived on.

This year's fall election is important, there's a lot at stake, people are paying more attention to who the candidates are and what they're saying. If we're lucky the winner will give people work, put us on a diet, pipe in sunshine, and send Britney back to childhood.

The Six Million Dollar Man

Thirty years ago American astronaut Steve Austin had a serious accident. As a result he underwent a costly operation with bionic replacements made for his right arm, both legs, and left eye. These parts enhanced his strength, speed, and vision. The cost: six million dollars.

Portrayed by Lee Majors in the ABC series, *The Six Million Dollar Man*, I've been thinking about Austin. I suspect it must have been a challenge getting used to his new body with all the increased powers in running, lifting, and seeing things. Be that as it may he kept his charming smile and took everything in stride. I think about Steve Austin as I get used to my new body, which is really the old body with decreasing powers in running, lifting, and seeing things.

While getting six million dollars in new parts is a plus, I am coping with the same old structure and that's a problem. Because many things have changed, and not for the better, I feel like I have a new body and it's not easy understanding how the beat goes on. I am also recuperating from ocular herpes, a definite set-back in the vision department and a disease that can make you feel older than you are. My skin isn't as pliant as it once was and has colored spots, scars keep accumulating, and gray hair is a give-away that I've passed more than a few summers. Muscular legs lack dedication for the long haul, back aches sometimes, and the battle of the bulge looks like my force is in full retreat.

I am learning through life what my Singapore doctor explained to me five years ago. Robert Don is a former U.S. Navy contract doctor who used to visit passing ships to treat injured sailors. As he explained it, *Medicine used to be easy when I treated young sailors, they usually broke bones and were easy to diagnose and treat; now it is hard as the young sailors have aged to become ancient mariners.* His comment made me laugh and I had to asked him if I'd reached ancient mariner status? Ever tactful, Doctor Don replied, *Of course not, what I mean is that when we're young the injuries are obvious, but as we age internal medicine comes more into play and that's when things get tricky.* Now my body feels as though it's in the tricky phase of Doctor Don's explanation to our lifecycle.

I am concerned not so much with the cosmetics of the outer shell of what I can see and whine about; it's the inside that is troubling. It's those organs like the heart, lungs, kidneys, liver, and brain, what's going on there that I can't see? How about the connectivity of nerves and blood vessels? Is there trouble ahead? What about bird flu, dengue fever, malaria, snake bite, hepatitis, and more herpes infections. What about my hearing? What about my girlfriend, she wants to dye my hair brown? But maybe she was joking! I can't remember now. Why can't I remember like I used to? Am I an ancient mariner?

I've also been thinking about losing my sight, ocular herpes is a serious disease that affects 25 million Americans, it can cause blindness. I am not hand-in-the-glove comfortable with blindness. As a small boy I used to live during the summers with my grandfather and grandmother, Bill and Opal Aper. They had a small farm in the countryside near Milan, Michigan. One of my pastimes was to watch my grandfather's Belgian gelding Dick in his day-to-day luxury of being put out to pasture. Dick was blind, but had a horse friend, his matched workmate, also a Belgian gelding named Dick. Blind Dick relied upon his seeing-eye stable friend, Dick, to guide him when needed.

In the world there are about 200 million people who are visually impaired, an estimated 40 million who are totally blind. Interestingly, 70-80 percent of those with visual impairment are that way because of malnutrition and preventable diseases. My grandmother developed cataracts in her 80s, eventually it led to blindness.

Murl Mae Welch was my other tough grandmother, she was a disciplinarian and it was from her that I learned I possessed a broad streak of independence. Besides being a strict overseer, grandma loved to read, it didn't matter if it were books, newspapers, or magazines. After blindness overtook her, she continued her quest for knowledge by listening to audio books. At about 90, she decided to have cataract surgery, which restored her sight for one day. Losing your sight twice in a lifetime is a tragedy we can scarcely imagine. Steve Austin had six million dollars in new parts, but he didn't have the heart power of my grandmother in facing adversity.

As an old blind woman she continued to live alone in her small home, cooking, cleaning, and taking care as best she could. My father, the angel, spent a lifetime honoring his mother and father. He was at his finest during her final years, most especially in guaranteeing that she was as comfortable as possible.

Because ocular herpes caused me to have these unique remembrances, you may also be interested to know that I was treated by the provincial hospital at Nakhon Phanom, population 32,000. I was a walk-in patient to the ophthalmology clinic, waited 30 minutes to be seen by a doctor, spent 15 minutes in conversation and tests. Doctor bill: $1.75 and three medications, $18.00. I wasn't treated better or worse than anyone else except that most Thais at the provincial hospital receive free medicine.

Nine days from the onset of the disease, my eyes are bloodshot and swollen, but vision is clear. I won't be going blind and am not aging faster than anyone else. I am lucky, especially in not having the six million dollar Steve Austin upgrade, can you imagine how much a tune-up would cost?

Teaching an Old Dog New Tricks

Teaching old dog new tricks requires good humor, patience, and persistence to believe that a miracle can occur if we try hard enough. If you are that old dog, the same principles apply. A month ago I was hired to be an English teacher at Suankularb Wittayalai School at Rangsit, a suburb north of Bangkok. In signing up with the school I joined 60-70,000 foreign teachers that work and live in Thailand. They, or rather we, are teaching everywhere in private, public, and specialized language schools; colleges and universities. Foreigners teach everything, but our specialty is English. The English teachers come from Australia, United Kingdom, New Zealand, America, Canada, South Africa, and the Philippines; other teachers from China, Taiwan, and Japan are presenting their languages. Learning to speak Chinese is increasingly popular everywhere around the world.

I don't always know or understand why people do the things they do and that includes my own motivation. I left a comfortable retirement: sleeping late, jogging in pristine countryside settings, taking a weekly tour of my rubber plantation, hours of reading, afternoon naps, and time for thinking. Perhaps there is such a thing as being too comfortable.

Since my daughter, Mary, entered kindergarten with Annie Murphy and Adrianna Reynolds as her teachers I've had an extremely high regard for the teaching profession. This high regard extends to awe of the value teaching brings to the world everywhere. Mary attended Hutchison Elementary School at Herndon, Virginia, and as a parent who often visited her class; I was left with a deep impression of the wonderful contribution good teachers make to academic and character excellence in kids. Now 16, Mary is continuing to be propelled forward by the momentum that Annie and Adrianna gave her in that first year.

Last fall, I was standing in line at the Thai Embassy at Vientiane, Laos, waiting to update my tourist visa. In line were several English teachers who described their profession in Thailand with conviction and passion. It seemed to me that they were making a positive difference in the lives of others and enjoying themselves, as well. The seed of an idea was planted.

In March, I attended an 120-hour course in Teaching English as a Foreign Language. It was conducted at Chiang Mai, Thailand, with the school, Siam Education Experience. Those four weeks included an association with ten inspiring classmates from America, Canada, England, and Ireland; instruction under a master of encouragement, Englishman John Quinn; and six hours of practice teaching to elementary school and university students. My classmates were young, extremely bright, and helpful to me in acquiring a more youthful spin on research, study, and teaching. After completing the course I applied to about 20 schools: four were interested. The first interview was with a private kindergarten to teach two to six-year olds. Although it was a lovely setting, I am fortunate not to have been selected for the job.

At the second session I was interviewed on a Sunday afternoon and as luck would have it I was hired to start work the next day. The third and fourth interviews with other schools were never scheduled.

My school, Suankularb Wittayalai (translation Rose Garden College) is the most famous public high school in Thailand. It was established by King Chulalongkorn on March 8, 1882, as the first public secondary school in the country. The original school was located near the rose garden at the Grand Palace and was created to teach royal page lieutenants. Later the curriculum changed from military studies to a more broad-based focus. There are now eight branches of Suankularb, the Rangsit School where I teach was built in 1995 and is, by far, the best-known and most respected government secondary school in Pathumthani Province.

The school has a strict dress code for faculty and well groomed students wear uniforms. I am assigned to the Foreign Language Department with five other English teachers, three Chinese teachers, several Japanese teachers, and Thai teachers who are presenting lessons in English grammar. My team of English teachers is from Austria, England, Philippines, and the U.S. We specialize in coaching students in correct pronunciation while increasing their vocabulary in reading and speaking. Everything is oral; there are no written examinations.

My teaching days start by riding my bicycle 20 minutes to school. On the country road to school I pass rice paddies, grazing cattle, and students traveling to the school. Upon arrival, I first stand at the front gate for an hour to greet faculty, parents, and students; attend the flag raising and playing of Thai national anthem and school song, and finally a Buddhist prayer. This is all conducted outdoors with 3,300 students and 160 teachers gathered together. After the prayer I visit an 11th grade class that I counsel. There are 50 kids in this class and I speak to them about some aspect of self-improvement.

My first class usually starts at 8:30 a.m., and the last concludes at 3:10 p.m. In a week I will teach 500 students in 20 different classes. The smallest classes are 20 kids and the largest at 50 students. Student behavior isn't perfect. From grades 7 through 12, the kids squirm, whisper, laugh, use mobile phones, listen to MP3s, and some of the more rambunctious jump around like monkeys. I spend five to ten minutes at the beginning of every class in disciplining students in such a fashion as they are not alienated or lose too much face with their classmates. As long as I am fair in getting them focused on their studies, the students will respond favorably including taking the time to rise and say, *thank you teacher*, at the end of every class.

Lunch is at the school cafeteria, for a dollar I can have some combination of spicy Thai foods such a rice, beef, pork, chicken, noodles, eggs, and vegetables. It is quite good. The building in which I teach is nine floors, there aren't enough elevators, so I often climb up or down, it's faster, more healthy, and tiring.

I am learning to connect student nickname with faces. I smile at the names: A, Arm, Ball, Beach, Bee, Beer, Bell, Best, Big, Bike, Bloom, Boat, Boom, Boss, Bow, Boy, Care, Cat, Champ, Cream, Dear, Dew, Dive, Dream, Drink, Earth, F, Fa (means blue), Fern, Few, Film, First, Gamey, Gap, Gift, Golf, Got, Ham, Ice, Ink, Jam, Jayjay, Jiji, Jett, Joy, Kong, Lek (means small), Look, Man, Milk, Mind, Mink, Mint, Mook, Moon, New, Next, Nice, Noi (means small), Noon, Nun, Nut, Pair, Palm, Paper, Pear, Pea, Pee, Ping, Pipe, Pla (means fish), Pond, Pop, Prince, Princess, Nok (means bird), Now, Oh, Time, Top, R-Po, Sea, Sent, Shake, Sky, Sunny, Stop, Star, Titan, Toon, Top, View, White, Win, Wow, Yo, and there is a Jack, Jane, Joe, June, Mark, May, Michelle, and Tom.

Being an old dog that learns new tricks is rewarding because of the student's high energy level, which rubs off on me; pleasant personalities of the Thai kids and faculty that make my days more enjoyable; and the opportunity to continue learning about culture from a different aspect of Thai society.

The Cowboy Way

As much as I travel the wonder of seeing the volume and diversity of exported American culture never ceases to amaze me. We export our lifestyle, heritage, democratic beliefs, good humor, and so much more through books, movies, music, and thousands of US multinational companies, which share technology, managerial style, and sense of fair play in the workplace.

Thailand's Chokchai Balakul grew up watching American western movies, and as he often good-naturedly conveyed to his family and friends, *I always wanted to be a cowboy.*

For a few years in my early life that's what I thought about, too. But I outgrew such thoughts after shoveling enough smelly cow and horse manure on my grandparent's farm to ensure that such ideas were just a phase I went through. Mr. Balakul didn't change his childhood notion of being a cowboy and as a result he came to set in motion a business empire that conveys America's western heritage.

Several weeks ago, I was fortunate to travel on a field trip with 11th graders at my school, Suankularb Wittayalai Rangsit School, to Chokchai Farm at Nakhon Ratchasima, 160 kms (100 miles) northeast of Bangkok, to see a fascinating Thai-American tradition at work.

With 8,000 acres and 5,000 cattle, Chokchai Farm is more than a dot on Thailand's business map. A construction contractor who worked for Americans in Southeast Asia building roads and airport runways, Mr. Balakul made his first modest land purchase of 100 acres in 1957. By 1969, the business was the largest and most advanced cattle ranch in Thailand and Chokchai opened the first of three steakhouses. In 1978, the company had developed a new dairy breed, the Chokchai Friesian by crossbreeding Sahiwal and Holstein Friesians from the Netherlands. This new breed of dairy cow proved most productive in Asia's tropical climate. Today 500 Chokchai Friesians are exported annually to China, Laos, and Vietnam.

In 1987, Chokchai Farm introduced pasteurized milk to Thailand's children. But all was not well on the horizon. Ten years later, the ranching operation experienced a downturn in prosperity along with the local economy. Nineteen ninety-seven was the year Thailand's over-extended economy perpetuated a global financial crisis by first spreading insecurity to other Asian countries, then to Europe, and America. In the aftermath, Chokchai Farm found itself 200 million baht in debt without a clear path to solvency. The result was a diversification of the cattle ranch to include selling the dairy operation and starting an agri-tourism operation using the ranch to teach and entertain. As the property became an educational playground, animal husbandry led to raising turkeys, ostriches, race horses, dogs, macaws, sheep, and other animals. Later a smaller dairy operation was started under the brand name, *Umm! Milk.*

Logistics at Chokchai's natural theme park are impressive; it has 2,000 milking cows that each gives 18 liters (4.75 gallons) of milk a day, in the aggregate that is 30 tons of milk. There are 3,000 calves, yearlings, and heifers. Everyday Chokchai livestock consume 120 tons of fresh grass, hay, corn, and fermented corn. The milkers are kept in comfortable and spacious paddocks where their high-quality diet is controlled; the younger cows are at pasture.

There are 250,000 visitors who take the 2-3 hour ranch tour every year to see quarterhorses, antique farm equipment, and cows along with Thai cowboys who wear leather chaps and broad-brimmed Western hats. They ride, crack whips, bulldog calves, twirl ropes, and do fast draw tricks. Guests can milk cows, sample ice cream, eat steak dinners, and ride all-terrain vehicles.

Touring the ranch is great entertainment and gives a splendid orientation to the Thai-American cowboy tradition along with insights into how we all come to enjoy milk and everyone's favorite, ice cream.

The land is in a beautiful setting with surrounding mountains, not Rocky Mountain-sized monuments, but smaller, tree covered hillocks that break the landscape giving refreshing views of what Mother Nature can provide on her best days. Because the land is at a higher elevation, temperatures are cooler, nearby farms raise grapes and silk worms. The area itself is popular for Khmer ruins, wildlife, waterfalls, and mountain forests where people ride horses and bicycles.

Now the Chokchai Business Group includes restaurants, boutique camping, ranching, real estate development, and the agri-tour. Not a bad heritage for a Thai man who found inspiration in the likes of our American western heroes: Gene Autry, Roy Rogers, John Wayne, and so many others.

Bridge Over the River Kwai

Those old enough to remember American actor William Holden (1918-1981) may also recall 1957's movie, *Bridge Over the River Kwai*. The movie won an Academy Award for Best Picture; Holden had won an Academy Award for Best Actor several years earlier in 1954. That movie was *Stalag 17*. I mention *Bridge Over the River Kwai* because it was an enthralling anti-war movie that used Thailand as an historical backdrop.

Bridge Over the River Kwai was a work of fiction based on the novel *Le Pont de la Riviere Kwai* by Frenchman Pierre Boulle. Boulle had been a French prisoner of war in Thailand and based his novel on the accurate historical setting in construction of the Thailand-Burma Railroad, also known as the Death Railway.

Construction of the railway was a Japanese war crime in the Asian Holocaust in which millions of civilians and POWs were killed.

The Japanese used about 260,000 conscripted Asian civilians and 60,000 POWs mainly from Australia, England, and Netherland. Of the 60,000 men, there were only about 700 Americans, but over 50 percent died working on the railway, an unusually high ratio compared to POWs from other countries. There is a Bridge Over the River Kwai, which fits the historical context of the movie and novel, except it is the Bridge Over the River Khwae Yai at the small town of Kanchanaburi, about 100 miles northeast of Bangkok.

At Kanchanaburi and the surrounding area there are museums, cemeteries, and other memorials to mark the brutalizing undertaking. Orchestrated by the Imperial Japanese Army, the railway was doomed from the start. In an aerial survey to determine the best route, the senior Japanese engineer, Lieutenant General Shimada Nobuo and 11 other senior officers, disappeared in an airplane crash. The terrain is still just as rugged as it was in 1942 as the plane wreckage and bodies have never been found. The result of this tragic accident was that junior engineers prepared a flawed construction plan that needlessly cost time and the lives of workers.

It is estimated that 100,000 civilians and 12-16,000 POWs died from starvation, untreated diseases, overwork, and brutality. While the bodies went to mass graves near railroad camps, the POWs were eventually reinterred into neatly maintained military cemeteries near the railroad. These cemeteries are maintained by the Commonwealth War Graves Commission. Three hundred and fifty-six American bodies were returned to the U.S. for burial. Historians theorize that civilian deaths were much higher because the civilians lacked the discipline of military POWs.

Of note, the Commonwealth War Graves Commission was started in 1917 as a nonprofit British organization. It now maintains 2,500 cemeteries in 150 countries for over one million military men and women killed in war.

A quick historical perspective: In 1942, a force of 25,000 Japanese soldiers overran the British force of 85,000 from the Malay Peninsula and Singapore, giving Great Britain its most crushing defeat in history. At about the same time, the Japanese conquered the Dutch East Indies (Indonesia). The end result was that Japan found itself with an unexpected 140,000 POWs, a convenient form of manpower that could help make their plans of a railroad from Bangkok, Thailand to Rangoon, Burma (now Myanmar) a reality. The railroad would be 415 kilometers (258 miles) long passing through such places as Hellfire Pass and Three Pagodas Pass. Purpose of the proposed railway was to move about 3,000 tons of supplies a day to provision an envisioned invasion of India and to maintain the war front in Burma. The railway connected an already existing line that ran from Singapore through Malaya and across Southern Thailand to Bangkok.

Taking the rugged jungle terrain into account, the first engineering study by the Japanese indicated it would take an estimated five years to complete the railroad. However, using brutality as motivation to move men beyond normal endurance the project was completed in 16 months. The cost was death. Every kilometer of track cost the lives of 38 POWs.

Started in October of 1942, the line was completed in August 1943. As a monument to the effort there are three military cemeteries: Kanchanaburi and Chungkai in Thailand, and Thanbyuzayat in Myanmar. Passing through the beautifully landscaped cemeteries is to be reminded of the indecency of cruelty that man can inflict on man. Many of the POW casualties were young men in their late teens and early twenties. They died from torture, malaria, cholera, and dysentery; lack of medical care; and overwork.

After the railway was completed, many civilians and a few POWs were reassigned to railroad maintenance and cutting wood to power the locomotives. Other POWs were transferred to Japan to work in mines and factories in support of the war effort, others were returned to the infamous Changi Prison at Singapore.

The British and Americans flew bombing missions over the line starting in December of 1944. Their targets were mainly bridges. Bridge Over the River Kwai, also known as Bridge 277, was of steel construction mounted on concrete pilings. The bridge had been disassembled in Java, Indonesia, and shipped to Thailand in pieces.

Major spans were destroyed by British and American bombing runs in February and April of 1944. On many of the numerous allied attempts to destroy bridges, POWs became casualties in the crossfire as bombs missed their targets and shrapnel from antiaircraft fire fell from the sky. In one instance, the Japanese lined Bridge 277 with allied POWs to discourage the allies from dropping bombs on the bridge. Sixty-eight POWs died as several spans of the bridge were destroyed.

In the best of times the railroad never reached the intended movement of 3,000 tons of supplies daily; 1,000 tons was the best they could manage.

Even as the Japanese surrendered and the war ended, the human destruction continued as many of the POWs were crippled for the rest of their lives. Others spent the rest of their days in hospitals. Some suffered mental problems, marriages were torn apart, and maybe the most tragic events were the suicides of men who had survived years of captivity and slavery.

The movie, *Bridge Over the River Kwai,* garnered seven Academy Awards. Besides Best Picture, awards were presented for Best Actor, Best Director, Best Screenplay, Best Score, Best Cinematography, and Best Film Editing.

A memorable feature of the film was a tune whistled by the POWs. Entitled, *The Colonel Bogey March*, it was a tune that typified British fortitude and dignity during times of privation. The lush Thai jungle scenery wasn't really Thai as the movie was made in Ceylon (now Sri Lanka), a large tropical island off the coast of Southern India. *Bridge Over the River Kwai* continues to be a highly watchable movie because of the compelling story and all-around excellence of production. If you haven't seen it recently it's available at www.amazon.com and other on-line sources.

Drama in Thailand

This is about the fascinating world of Thailand. The population of 63-million live in an area the size of California or France, and just as everywhere else life is complicated.

The people are embroiled in as much drama as anywhere on earth. As a third world, developing country immersed in globalization, the Thai people are torn between tradition and ways of the future. Poor farming families are leaving the land to be part of the country's industrial revolution; the children are becoming young adults, going to universities and slowly taking their positions with the international community. There are still plenty of poor people, but the trend is toward more prosperity.

The Kingdom of Thailand is an interesting place for an expatriate to live. There are few dull moments and the day-to-day events keep me wondering and growing as I learn more about the Asian world.

The King of Thailand, Bhumibol Adulyadej is 80 and the oldest living monarch, he's also been on the job longer than any of the other international royals. If all the kings and queens in the world were put into one palace and their wealth counted, the King of Thailand would come out on top with 35 billion dollars. He and his family are highly respected because they do an absolutely splendid job of supporting the people. They have used resources wisely by spearheading 3,000 projects that lift standards of life among the rural poor.

As a democratic-monarchy, there is another side to the equation and that is people support by the democratically elected parliament. Unfortunately, that government power center doesn't function as well. It is dominated by corrupt, populist politicians who don't always have the best interest of the people at heart.

Disappointment and frustration have recently been overflowing with protesters calling for the resignation of the Prime Minister, Samak Sundaravej. He was eventually brought down from office because of ethical violations in his hosting of two television cooking shows (I am not making this up).

Since taking office seven months ago, the prime minister had been clueless to the professional responsibilities of his office. He appointed corrupt cronies into his administration's key positions, shunned the media, and presented an arrogant public persona. One of Thailand's major political parties, The People's Alliance for Democracy (PAD), protested for his resignation by occupying seven government buildings for a couple of weeks, several people were killed during public protests by an opposing political party in counter protests. The police and army monitored events closely.

Now that Samak has been court-removed from office, his party, The People's Party, is nominating him a second time to be prime minister, a move that has caused widespread irritation with ministers in parliament.

In the parliament, Democratic Minister Malinee Sukvejworakij, who is a doctor of medicine, said Prime Minister Samak showed symptoms of a mental deficiency and behavioral disorder. She continued that he has done a few things that would indicate he has a low IQ and emotional quotient. Samak countered that he is not crazy. And so it goes...

Democracy was introduced in Thailand in 1934, since that time there have been 19 successful coups to overthrow the governing politicians. Because of the head-of-steam driving protesters and the prime minister's inflexibility, it would appear that a coup, bloodless or otherwise, is on the horizon.

Besides the political crisis, which has resulted in declaration of a State of Emergency by the Samak government, the Thai people have been jostled by increased food and energy costs, a frustrating border dispute with Cambodia, a continuing and serious terrorism threat in three southern provinces, and slowed economic development driven by events in the world's developed nations. Tourism accounts for six percent of the national income, 25 countries have issued travel advisories against travel to Thailand because of the potential for violence, and income from tourism is down about 30 percent. Tourism to Bangkok has been reduced from 120,000 people a day to 80,000.

Outside of the rough and tumble world of political conflict life is continuing in an interesting fashion: Legislators at the seat of national government in Bangkok have passed a law focused on helping the poorest members of Thai society. It is a six-point plan that cuts taxes for diesel fuel and gasohol, provides free electricity and water for small households, free buses for Bangkok residents, and free third-class train travel. I now save six dollars a month by receiving free water at my home. The government has also introduced a bill to license beggars. This new law would require beggars to register and carry their ID cards when going about their "work."

This is the rainy season and flooding has been especially bad along the Mekong River Valley. Experts on water control attribute the flooding to China, which has constructed three large dams that artificially control water flows. Efforts to communicate with the Chinese on this issue have not been particularly fruitful. The Mekong River is 1,250 miles in length, 465 miles are in Thailand where it defines the border between Laos and Thailand before entering Cambodia and finishing its journey in Vietnam by flowing into the South China Sea.

At Samut Prakan, a suburban province (provinces are county equivalents) of Bangkok, 499 Buddhist, Christian, Islamic and Hindu priests recently gathered to pray against an expected storm surge in October. The surge is expected as a result of strong onshore winds, low-lying land, and heavy rains.

Also in the province, Mr. Choochat Dulayapraphatsom, has been elected as a village chief. Mr. Choochat, also called Je Kob, or older sister, is a transvestite and received the most votes because of his many years of service to the community. Thailand's plastic surgeons are among the best practiced in the world in altering body parts. The transvestite community is estimated to range from 10,000 to 100,000, in other words, nobody knows for sure.

Teen violence is on the rise and headlined with several teens recently involved in murder. Worst was a lad who needed money to feed his addiction to video games. He tried to support his habit by robbing an elderly taxi driver. The event went wrong, the driver is dead. In another incident, a ninth grader stabbed to death an 11th grader who had repeatedly taunted and spat on him. From a student population of 14 million there have been 3,000 incidents of student fighting in the past 11 months--high by Thai standards, but extremely low by experience in developed nations. Social scientists attribute these acts to violent films and news reports, game machines, computer games, the Internet, TV programming, novels, and cartoons. No surprises there. Thailand is also a permissive society where children are raised on pure kindness with less regard toward discipline.

Three provinces (Pattini, Yala, and Narathiwat) in South Thailand suffer terribly from terrorism violence. Sadly, the insurgency is a separatist campaign with Islamic terrorists attempting to influence a breakaway from Buddhist Thailand. They target teachers, school principals, government workers, monks, Buddhist villagers, police, and soldiers with students caught in the crossfire. The death toll is now at 3,000 from about 7,000 acts of violence in the past 5 years.

And the drama continues...

With Yong and Pang in Thailand

Last Saturday morning I had an excellent day as a school teacher. Excellent days happen to me with regularity because of my environment, which is filled with an adventure every hour in my school's classrooms. On the day in question, September 27, I had been asked to officiate at a district spelling bee in English that was being held among eight high schools. In the week leading up to the contest, I was also coaching three 11th grade students that would appear in other competitions. Nusara Jekhoggruad (short name Yong) and Sophida Boonbutra (short name Pang), were in the English quiz, and Dutfun Kradasthong (short name Bhumbhim), was a storytelling contestant.

I drilled Yong, 16, and Pang, 15, for three hours on English culture, current events, geography, politics, and economics. Brighter than tropical sunlight at midday, they were exquisite in their curious nature and ability to absorb knowledge. Although they had never traveled out of Thailand they were worldly because of two things: television news and the Internet. Both girls offered that they surf the net about two hours a day, chatting with friends in different countries, and generally learning a little about the world every day. The English quiz is really a place for geeks: kids that wear Coke bottle glasses, don't smile much, and do mental cartwheels at the prospect of reading another book. Not these girls, they have 20/20 vision without glasses; spend an inordinate amount of time smiling, giggling or laughing; and don't let their weighty brains bowl them over in social settings.

For the spelling bee, there were 16 contestants, four judges and one official who read the words and a descriptive sentence to illustrate word meaning--that was my assignment. In the first round of 25 words, 12 contestants bite the dust, of the four remaining students one was from my school, Suankularb Wittayalai Rangsit School. Words used in the contest were drawn from a pool of words submitted by the schools. Examples of words used: cassette, relax, interesting, daughter, homework, headache, and plain. Although these are not hard words for school students who speak English as a native language, foreigners find them challenging.

We went through a second round of 25 words, and two more contestants dropped including the great young lady from my school. I administered the third round of ten words and as fate had intended one student was supreme.

After the spelling bee, there was a quick snack of rice, beef, and a spicy Thai sauce to warm the innards from burning tongue and throat downward. Then I became a spectator at the English quiz with Yong and Pang. There were eight two-person teams, many of these kids knew their stuff and it was obvious that their mental prowess was a force to be reckoned with. This is the right time to emphasize that these kids didn't know about Yong and Pang. There are times in life when we find ourselves hopelessly overmatched by a friend, family member, co-worker, or spouse who has brainpower on their side. There would be more harmony in the world if God would just give us all the same mental equipment, but for reasons known only to Him that doesn't happen. Be that as it may, I have experience at being mismatched with people around me and if you find yourself in that kind of frustrating position, believe me, I understand.

There were two rounds with 20 questions in each session. Yong and Pang, working as a team, made their competitors look bad; some of them were young men. I felt sadness for them as I gave inner cheers for both genders. Yong and Pang knew that the Thai media refers to America's economic problems as the *hamburger crisis*; no one else in the room knew that, not even the teachers. They also knew that the Bangkok subway was completed in 2004, no one else knew that either. And then there was the question no one knew the answer to: In a rainbow, what color appears between orange and green? After the contest, I was invited to have my picture taken with the two super stars who easily won the contest. My remark at the time: *It's interesting how the students do all the work and teachers jump into the picture.* The students laughed loudly; teachers laughed less loud; I smiled.

Through no fault of her own, Bhumbhim came in second in a field of two. Her fable, *White Spirit Cloud, the Sand God, and the Moon Goddess* was an excellent choice, and her gestures and vocal quality were exceptional, but as sometimes happens she received poor coaching from a teacher to recite the story verbatim, a difficult task without more time to practice. My direction to be spontaneous had been trumped by a Thai teacher under-qualified to coach storytelling.

Besides the spelling bee, English quiz, and storytelling, the Saturday program included a *Scrabble* competition, called *Crossword* in Thailand; fruit and vegetable carving, traditional dancing, and well-conceived displays explaining complicated scientific principles. The kids were excited, nervous, and happy with their competition; the teachers cheerful and supportive; it was a good day for me, one of many I experience as a teacher. Now I am not only richer for having spent a Saturday with children, but I know about the *hamburger crisis* and to use more caution with spicy Thai sauces that burn from tongue to throat and then all the way down.

Vietnam, Yesterday and Today

Smell the rice, noodles, and spices simmering in sidewalk cookery, hear the hum of motorbikes, watch energetic people with cone hats, and feel the cool fall breeze beside a pretty lake. Welcome to a taste of Vietnam as experienced through a week in Hanoi.

Vietnam is one of those tantalizing pieces of real estate that everyone loves. The Chinese loved it so much that when they invaded they stayed 1,000 years notwithstanding invitations to go back where they came from. Then the French came in 1847 for an unwelcome colonization until the Japanese arrived as another uninvited guest. The Land of the Rising Sun people were booted out at the end of World War II, to be replaced again by the French. The Viet Minh, an army organized around nationalism and communism was finally able to physically evict the French after an embarrassing military defeat at the Battle of Diem Bien Phu in 1954.

But wait, there's more. France's good friend America wanted to visit and arrived through Vietnam's backdoor in the southern city of Saigon. Then we see 25 years of America's presence for better or worse as they say in many marriage vows. But the union wasn't a happy one and the split resulted in Vietnam now being occupied only by the Vietnamese people, which makes them happy and seems to make sense.

As the foreign powers arrived, occupied and departed, lives were lost on all sides, but it was mainly the Vietnamese and neighboring Cambodians and Laotians who lost the vast number of people: soldiers and civilians. The loss of life, disruption of communities, destruction of historic monuments and architectural treasures, and the environmental damage is astounding. I mention this because today's enthusiastic welcoming of foreigners is the trademark of forgiveness,

205

resiliency, and strength in a people who seemingly never give up.

Walking Hanoi streets I saw remarkable French architecture and small mountains of delicious freshly-baked French breads and pastries (yum, yum), crossed busy streets filled with brightly painted Honda and Suzuki motorbikes, and heard American pop music floating out of cafes and restaurants. And the Chinese, they are in the architecture of temples and pagodas, and the faces of the Vietnamese. While Vietnam is an economic Asian tiger, China is the dragon that everyone respects.

In Hanoi as well as Saigon (Ho Chi Minh City), many residents speak English and they like to find foreigners to converse with. When they learn I am from the America they asked about Barack Obama for president and Bill and Hillary Clinton who had a good visit there in 2000. I tell them about John McCain, his five years as a POW in Hanoi and his work to improve trade relationships and help Vietnamese immigrants in the United States, most don't know about that.

Officially known as the Socialist Republic of Vietnam, the country is only communist in name and censorship of the media. Led by Saigon's inspiring commercial successes, communism is no longer meaningful to the government or the people. In a country of 84 million, Saigon has only eight million people but produces 40 percent of the national income. Their economy, based on free enterprise, has been expanding at an impressive eight to nine percent in recent years. That prosperity is funding a building spree of large proportion. Everywhere you see public works construction in new roads, bridges, and civic buildings. The number of new and well-maintained homes painted in pretty pastels, shiny new Japanese cars, and upscale boutiques suggest that being part of economic globalization is good for everyone.

The memory of Ho Chi Minh (1890-1969) holds the number one spot in the hearts of the Vietnamese. He is their national hero and a man for all seasons: a kindly and humble man who believed in simplicity, he rose to prominence as the leader who successfully fought against the French, Japanese, and American forces occupying his country. Known as Uncle Ho for his gentle nature, love of children, and quiet demeanor; his exemplary life as a revolutionary and government leader is well assured in Vietnam's history books. The hearts of the Vietnamese also go to their patriot soldiers who fought generation after generation to liberate the country from foreigners. There are monuments everywhere to their sacrifice.

Vietnam is a youth-oriented country. With 84 million people it is the 13th most populace country in the world. Amazingly, 65 percent of the people are under age 30 and that means city streets and country lanes are filled with kids at joyful play as well as pursuing serious efforts at education: primary, secondary, and university studies. Universities are packed, Hanoi homes are wired for the Internet, and globalization is quickly changing Vietnam's personality.

As in Thailand and Malaysia, which have both had major shifts in population from agriculture and country living to employment in the nation's cities, the Vietnamese migration is bringing prosperity and new lines of thought that extend beyond national borders. University students optimistically talk about studying, living, and working abroad. Vietnam is also a country of contrasts, almost two nations divided between the rich and poor, north and south, urban vs. rural residents, and an older, more traditional generation patiently trying to understand today's feisty youth culture that is adopting international norms. Family structure continues to be important and wondrous to Westerners as they see three generations living under one roof.

Religion in Vietnam is a mix of Buddhism, Taoism, Confucianism, and Christianity. Buddhism has two varieties, one in the north and a separate system of beliefs in the south. Northern monks wear brown, southern monks wear yellow. They both worship in homes and pagodas. Temples are used for ancestor and hero worship. For example, there are temples devoted to Confucius, Ho Chi Minh, patriot soldiers, and ancient rulers of the country. Pagodas are devoted to the worship of Buddha. Taoism is a philosophy that emphasizes contemplation and simplicity while Confucianism is an ethical code that promotes personal obligations to family, society, and country. Christianity is prominent in Vietnam through Catholicism. There are also Muslims and Hindus, seemingly something for everyone. Many of these beliefs overlap one into another with people worshipping Buddha, but also devoting themselves to honoring ancestors and following the ethical standards established by Confucius.

There you have a snapshot of the history, lifestyle, and religion that I learned about during an exquisite week visiting Hanoi's temples, pagodas, and museums; walking the streets, sitting in parks, and most importantly, listening to people. The quality of the people we meet and associate with makes all the difference in our own sense of well being. Being part of their society, even in a small way, for my one week was an enrichment not to be forgotten.

My gateway to Vietnam was through Hanoi, which is an easy get-away from my home in Bangkok with a relatively inexpensive flight taking less than two hours. There are few countries as downright exciting as Vietnam. It is that way because of the high quality of the people (ambitious, friendly, fun and persistent), French colonial history along with a thousand-year occupation by China, and extreme scenic beauty. Every step of my journey was spellbinding.

After arrival at Hanoi's Noi Bai Airport I made my way to the Astoria Hotel on Hang Bong Street in the Old Quarter. My taxi driver was persistent in overcharging my fare by 50 percent, I laughed and gave him 320,000 dong (about $20), which was the proper amount plus tip. He grumbled, smiled, and we both moved on.

At the Astoria Hotel I met the hotel manager; Thuy Linh, the smart receptionist and tour coordinator; as well as the other staff members. It was easy to meet everyone as the Astoria has only 20 rooms. For $27 a day, I received a clean room with cable TV, unlimited Internet usage, and a substantial American breakfast. The Astoria is a two-star hotel with a five-star personality.

Before even seeing my room, Linh was entertaining me with ideas for tours during my stay. I couldn't resist the city tours (pagodas, temples, and museums), which are always a good idea no matter what new city you find yourself in. Seeing a city's best features gives you a bearing for your stay helping to develop appreciation for the people, their culture, and history. I selected my tours, pre-paid, and then checked out the room, which more than met my expectations.

The Old Quarter of Hanoi is known as 36 Pho Phuong (36 streets). The area has more charm and energy on its 36 narrow lanes than all of the remainder of Hanoi put together. Interestingly, the Old Quarter is over 600 years old as an artisan's district with crafts and trades concentrated on the 36 streets. My hotel was located on Hang Bong Street, which means Cotton Street because that's where clothing and material is sold. Silver workers are found on Pho Hang Bac (Silver Merchandise Street), basket weavers make their home on Hang Bo (bamboo basket merchandise), and so it goes.

The Old Quarter's narrow streets are intense with motorbike, bicycle, and pedestrian traffic. Adding color to the rainbow are cone-hatted ladies mostly in traditional garb selling fruit. They commute to the Old Quarter from outlying villages to supplement the family's agricultural income and like every other merchant I chanced upon they were tough in their unyielding enthusiasm to sell something.

After getting settled at the hotel, I took a stroll east on Hang Bong Street to Hang Da Street stopping at a pho shop (a few small plastic tables and tiny stools on the sidewalk). I had passed several quaint restaurants, but my preference is to dine where the working people eat and that's on the street. This is how the Vietnamese eat their fast food: outdoors, informally and in closeness to one another. I had one of my favorites in Asia, Pho Ga (chicken noodle soup) and was happily surprised that it didn't make me sneeze, sweat, or burn my throat. For a moment I had forgotten I wasn't in Thailand, but that doesn't mean Pho Ga has a boring taste, on the contrary it was out of this world with a tasty blend of chicken, rice noodles, fresh herbs and onions.

The passing scene was marvelous. It was evening and there was a steady stream of moving people on motorbikes and bicycles. It was noisy, but not unpleasantly so. Sitting just a few feet from the curb, riders who noticed me eating like a Vietnamese smiled with some taking a second look. The bowl of soup was large and delicious, but small in price at 10,000 dong (about 60 cents).

After my leisurely meal I struck out on a walk through the Old Quarter ultimately arriving at the intersection of Hang Trong and Le Thai To, which is a major tourist artery beside Ho Hoan Kiem (Lake of the Restored Sword or Turtle Lake).

It was at this location that I was approached by a woman claiming to be a Lady of the Night and she wanted me. She was pear-shaped and stretched the seams of her black spandex bodysuit. Her hair wasn't pretty, she was older, and was quick in publicly grabbing my buttocks. I protested disinterest, she persisted. Passersby didn't seem to notice anything out-of-the-ordinary. Finally, she touched my crotch and asked if I'd come back and see her tomorrow. With a thought that this might get rid of her I readily agreed that tomorrow would be best, she smiled and took her departure as well as my wallet. Within seconds I touched my right front pocket, that's the pocket where I carry my wallet in big cities but alas it was too late. My pear-shaped Lady of the Night was a just-pretend prostitute who used her make-belief occupation to cleverly get close, touch me, and deftly lift the merchandise. She was out-of-sight.

If you can imagine my position: I am in a strange city on my first day of a week-long vacation completely broke and not a credit card to my name. As I pondered my predicament, a cyclo driver pulled up offering to give me a lift. I told him he could take me to the Astoria Hotel, but I had no money. He didn't understand, laughed, and said he'd be glad to comply. After 15-minutes of pedaling we arrived at the hotel, and he asked for 100,000 dong (about $6 and more than double the usual fare). I told him he'd get whatever I could bum from the hotel desk clerk. He frowned. I explained to the clerk my predicament of being broke with a cyclo driver waiting for his fare. The clerk readily advanced me 55,000 dong; I passed it to the driver. He protested; I smiled, touched his arm, and told him in my most calming voice, *don't worry about it*. He seemed to understand!

After a sleepless night of wondering how I came about being one of the poorest rich men in Hanoi, the sun rose on a new day. I called my friend Pham Chuong Dai in Ho Chi Minh City. After explaining my sad situation and before I could ask, she said, *Larry, I'm so sorry this had to happen to you. I'll wire you 7,000,000 dong (about $425) tomorrow when my bank opens.* Dai is a catering supervisor at the five-star Caravelle Hotel. Although she is a well-paid professional, I suspect that this was her life savings. Vietnam is not a country of rich people. After the call, I told the hotel manager about Dai's generosity and asked him to advance me money for one day's expenses. He gave me 500,000 dong ($30), which allowed me to tour the city and continue to enjoy bowls of Pho Ga.

After transacting this bit of face-saving financial aid, I toured Hanoi for a full eight hours seeing a fascinating array of temples, pagodas, and museums; the Ho Chi Minh Tomb and his simple home; and the impressive Presidential Palace.

That evening I sent a text message to my friend Napaporn Wonghajak in Thailand. A village farm girl living near Nakhon Phanom, I told her about the pickpocket, she wrote back that she'd like to wire me 15,000 baht (about $440/7,269,000 dong). Once again I didn't ask for help, I know she is not rich, and this was probably most if not all of her savings. The next day I went to the bank and collected both transactions which gave me a full financial recovery. That allowed me to continue touring, shopping, and most importantly, eating.

This bitter-sweet story reflects how quickly our well-being can change and how important solid relationships are to survival when things go wrong. To say that I am blessed with the right kind of relationships is an understatement. I was humbled by this experience, first to lose everything, and secondly to have two such good friends bail me out. What these two young women knew is that if our circumstances were reversed I would be the White Knight riding to their rescue. Isn't that the way good friends take care of one another?

Frankly speaking, I live in paradise. Many millions of tourists save for eleven months of the year in order to spend several weeks seeing the world where I live. It isn't just Vietnam, but also the other ten countries that comprise Southeast Asia: Brunei, Cambodia, East Timor, Indonesia, Laos, Malaysia, Myanmar, Philippines, Singapore, and Thailand.

While in Hanoi, I enjoyed the rain, which is part of the charm of Southeast Asia. Rainfall is particularly interesting when observing the passing scene of motorbikes with riders covered in colorful plastic slickers and cone-hatted ladies selling fruit. There are also soggy kids taking a curious glance at the camera-clad foreigner who didn't seem to have enough sense to come in out of the rain. Just before the rainfall faded to a mist, I met Nguyen Lan and her friend Khanh, both university students and models of not only Vietnamese beauty, but also graciousness and good humor. They had taken shelter beneath a store awning. A smile led to a conversation as it often does when friendly Americans meet friendly foreigners. Both were seniors studying business management at one of Hanoi's many universities.

The following morning I was off on eight-hours of touring pagodas, temples, and museums; seeing Ho Chi Minh's Tomb, the Presidential Palace, and other fascinating sights that included an excellent repast at the Lady Bird Caffe on Hang Buom Street. The Lady Bird is one of Hanoi's most popular eateries for tourists as they serve a wonderful sampling of Vietnamese foods. That day-long tour gave me an anchor of appreciation for Vietnamese culture and history as well as a sense of geography for the contours of lakes and a major river that define Hanoi.

The first stop on my tour was Chua Tran Quoc, Vietnam's most ancient pagoda dating from 545. It is located on a scenic peninsula at West Lake, one of 18 lakes that bring unusual beauty to Hanoi. West Lake is the largest at about 1,000 acres. Water is an important design element in pagodas as well as water lilies, symbolic of peace.

Hanoi has many charming characteristics: people, food, architecture, and things that are old. The Van Mieu (Temple of Literature) was built in 1070 and dedicated to Confucius. In 1076, the temple was joined with the Quoc Tu Giam (School of the Elite of the Nation--Vietnam's first university). The school provided the genesis for training of mandarins who were Vietnam's government administrators. Students seated at this table of learning dined on philosophy, and ancient Chinese and Vietnamese history. Every three years a rigorous examination was conducted with high scorers being awarded a doctorate degree and assignment to a senior government post, those who failed the examination were sent back to their village to seek redemption and make their living as a teacher. In the 700 years in which the university functioned as a center of education, 2,313 doctorate degrees were awarded.

Chinese influence on Vietnam's culture is reflected in temple architecture and Chinese characters are common features of religious buildings.

Stone tablets are part of a collection of 117 that sit on the back of stone tortoises. The tablets, referred to as stelae, are inscribed with the names, works, and academic records of 1,306 scholars who succeeded in the 82 examination sessions held between 1442 and 1779. Of special interest, American Express funded preservation of the stones.

The Temple of Literature was dedicated to Confucius for good reason. Born in 550 B.C., he lived at a time of great political turmoil to become one of the foremost thinkers in human history. His genius proved to be as a strong moral and ethical guide who promoted a social order based on compassion, etiquette, loyalty, knowledge, and trust. For over 2,000 years Confucianism has been a pillar of the Vietnamese moral and spiritual world. Confucius changed the way people think about compassion, honesty, humanity, loyalty, relationships, and sincerity. The moral code developed by Confucius influenced change around the world, but nowhere more prominently than in the East Asia countries of China, Korea, Japan, Vietnam, and Singapore. Although Confucius is worshipped, Confucianism is not a religion. Buddhists, Christians, Muslims or Zoroastrians can and do follow not only their own creed, but also the moral direction developed by Confucius.

My enjoyment of the Temple of Literature concluded with a traditional music concert presented by musicians who were especially skilled in folk music and instrumentation. They played lutes, fiddles, a zither, bamboo xylophone, and hammered dulcimer; and sang poetic songs about love, hard work, and tragedy, familiar topics in many countries of the world.

It was just a hop, skip, and a jump from the Temple of Literature to Ho Chi Minh's Tomb and Chua Mot Cot (One Pillar Pagoda). The tomb is a massive marker to the life of a simple man and although Ho Chi Minh would have opted for something more modest, the Communist government would have nothing less than a high-toned monument.

Contrary to his wish to be cremated, Ho Chi Minh's embalmed corpse lies in a glass casket in this monumental tomb. Uncle Ho, as he is affectionately known in Vietnam, is the country's foremost hero for his leadership and nearly a lifetime of struggle to liberate Vietnam from foreign domination.

Chua Mot Cot was originally built in 1049, with the wooden pagoda resting on a single concrete pillar rising out of a lotus pool. It was recently reconstructed after departing French soldiers blew it up in 1954. It was built by King Ly Thai To as a tribute to his young peasant wife who bore him a male heir.

Ban Tang Dan Toc Hoc Viet Nam (Vietnam Museum of Ethnology), is a treasure. Hanoi's newest and most modern museum, the main building and surrounding grounds are dedicated to explaining the fascinating life of Vietnam's 54 ethnic groups. The grounds are filled with strolling school children, their teachers, tourists, and wedding parties. Apparently, the picturesque grounds with its diversity of structures, meandering waterways, and tropical foliage make splendid backdrops for brides and bridegrooms in creating a lasting memory through the talents of professional photographers.

The museum recreates life among Vietnam's 54 minority groups. The displays describe births, deaths, weddings, art, culture, religion, and lifestyles of these people who live anywhere from river deltas to mountainous terrain. One of the major minority groups is the Black Thai, which is the second largest group with over a million people concentrated in Son La and Lai Chau Provinces.

While enjoying my stroll around the grounds I met university students taking a tourist survey as part of their studies. The names behind the smiles were Tuyet (means snow), Hanh (Happy) and Ha (River). All of the girls were majoring in tourism and filling a class requirement to learn what impressions Vietnam visitors were drawing from their stay.

The days touring concluded with visits to Ho Chi Minh's home, and the Presidential Palace, one a simple two room home on stilts, the other an ornate example of French colonial architecture.

Later in the week, I took a tour into the countryside near the city of Ninh Binh, which is about 55 miles southeast of Hanoi. On this tour I saw one additional historic pagoda, took a six mile bicycle ride through some of the most gorgeous scenery on earth, topping that with a fine Vietnamese lunch, and boat ride on the Ngo Dong River.

The Ngo Dong River trip was extraordinary. The river is located about 50 miles southeast of Hanoi near the small city of Ninh Binh. Best parts of boat rides are not paddling, seeing scenic beauty, and finding something to laugh about. As good luck would have it, the flat-bottomed boat was staffed by a pair of good humored helmsmen, a 30ish woman and teenage boy.

Helmsman Chu Thi Mai, 30, mother of two and the wife of a boat builder, was our guide and primary means of propulsion. Every day she rows passengers 12 miles to earn about three dollars. Seated behind her is a teenaged apprentice.

The area is spectacular with limestone mountains that are prominent in this region of Vietnam, even extending into the Gulf of Tonkin where they make an impressive series of 1,600 islands in Ha Long Bay, a World Heritage site.

Departing from the river village of Van Lam, for several hours we were carried into a tranquil world of freshness and quiet with a backdrop of mountains, rice paddies, playful ducks, and pleasant people. Along the way we passed through Tam Coc (Three Caves). These caves, known as grottoes in Italy, are watery tunnels that pass beneath the area's limestone mountains. Between the three caves were interesting limestone formations, quiet lagoons, herons, and a few fishermen. Inside the grottoes there are naturally beautiful stalactites and stalagmites.

Half-way through our boat tour local villagers in boats were gathered to tempt travelers with snacks and soft drinks.

216

Although many of them spoke excellent English, *No thank you*, didn't register in their lexicon. Later in the trip, our helmsman Mai stopped progress to do personal selling of embroidered table clothes, t-shirts, and handkerchiefs. She surprised me and although a bit overboard with her persistence I admired her enterprise and we laughed together about her captive customers. Mai thought my humor was more inspiring after I made several purchases.

The aluminum boats held up to three passengers plus the helmsmen and her assistant. The one good friend I made on the scenic waterway was Tran Ngoc, 24, a Hanoi university student studying to become an accountant. Ngoc's English was excellent and she possessed typical Vietnamese curiosity about the world and especially America.

After returning to the boat dock, I moved to a bicycle seat and set off on a six mile trek across the countryside. The freedom, cool and misty breeze, and stunningly beautiful scenery made me feel like a million dollars. I passed ponds, streams, rice paddies, limestone karsts, and lovely people. The kids were especially endearing. As I took photographs they charged me a pen or pencil, which I luckily had in my backpack. People waved and smiled as if to show they were genuinely pleased to see a foreigner in their midst.

Not far from the Ngo Dong River I chanced upon a smiling brother and sister team, also riding their bicycles. All of us stopping in the little used country lane, the kids spoke in English to ask my name and where I was from. After our small talk, I took their photograph and neither Van, 14, nor her brother Ziang, 10, cared to charge me a pen or pencil for their picture.

I also chanced upon the temple Den Tho Vua Dinh Tien Hoang; it has been rebuilt several times since initial construction a thousand years ago, most recently after being destroyed during the Vietnam War.

Later the mist turned to a light rain and those cone-hatted people I encountered were attired in colorful plastic slickers. Although soggy, I was refreshed by the experience.

Returning to Hanoi by rented van, bedtime came early as I reflected on one of my most perfect days as a tourist in Vietnam.

Probably my greatest thrill in Hanoi came from visiting 66A Nghia Dung Street in the Ba Dinh District. That's where I found The Blue Dragon Children's Foundation.

There I met the organization's founder and director, Michael Brosowski and his key aides Nadine Ziegeldorf and Amy Cherry. While Michael and Nadine are Australians, Amy is a school teacher from the United States. These three along with other staff members make you proud to be a human being when you see the TLC they administer to down-and-out kids. When I say down-and-out, I mean the worst sorts: victims of poverty with all that that means – human trafficking, commercial and sexual exploitation, drug abuse, malnutrition, untreated illnesses, and school drop-outs.

If you have children in your life, think about how vulnerable they are. In SE Asia, escaping the poverty cycle is nearly impossible for children, especially those living without families in a big city. That is why Blue Dragon and the personalities who drive it are such blessing.

The kids at Blue Dragon come with suitcases of need: education, health care, counseling, drug rehabilitation, and regular sleep and meals. Blue Dragon provides all that along with love, respect, and encouragement. In short, kids are made to feel human. From 8 to 80, all of us need emotional support to function well. Michael and his crew are doing amazing work in that regard.

I am enamored with Blue Dragon and Michael because of the concepts at work. Michael came to Hanoi in 2002 to teach English at Hanoi University, he saw the grind of poverty on homeless children and took steps to improve their world as best he could. Can one person make a difference? Absolutely,

Michael has proven that. From a most humble beginning Blue Dragon now has 30 paid Vietnamese staff and foreign volunteers who are making a most important difference in the lives of children. Two of the staff are totally dedicated to locating and rescuing children of human trafficking. Typically, they are poor rural children ages eight to fifteen who are sometimes sold into slavery by desperate parents.

Interestingly, Blue Dragon has the only Child Care Advocates in Vietnam. As with most developing countries who are finding success in globalization, Vietnam is making progress across the economic board, but the overwhelming social needs will take many years to resolve with the protection of women and children not high on the priority list.

If Blue Dragon sounds familiar to you, remember that when you purchased my book, *Quotations for Positive People*, the royalties went to benefit these unfortunate kids. Touring the Blue Dragon facility, one of several in Hanoi, visitors see the computer lab donated by the Government of Ireland in 2006. The equipment makes for a powerful teaching tool to bring kids into the age of globalization. There are also classes in food preparation and kids are apprenticed out to learn motorcycle mechanics.

Walls are filled with art and handicrafts made by the students. In addition to the in-house participants who live within Blue Dragon walls, there is a large population of neighborhood kids who arrive mornings for a day of games, tutoring in a variety of school-related topics, and warm, wholesome meals.

Since Blue Dragon was created it has attracted benefactors among Hanoi's international community from embassies to restaurants and hotels that focus on a global clientele. Employees of these institutions donate money, but just as valuable is the time they freely give to help in the childhood development of Blue Dragon kids.

In 2004, I observed for myself the plight of street children. While in Hanoi on business I was in the park beside Hoan Kiem Lake, a popular location for tourists in the Old Quarter. Sitting on a park bench I watched two policemen shake down a young teenager selling maps, books, postcards, and chewing gum to tourists. She was a poor girl just scrapping by. After the robbery, she sat on a nearby bench and I heard her sadly mutter through tears: *Why did I have to be born in Vietnam?* Sad, indeed! Thanks to Blue Dragon and other child advocacy groups things are better for many Vietnamese children, but the sheer numbers of these kids are overwhelming. We need to and can do better.

The Roi Nuac Thang Long (Thang Long Water Puppet Theater) is located on the corner of Dinh Tien Hoang in the Old Quarter of Hanoi. Water puppetry is uniquely Vietnamese. It was created hundreds of years ago along the Song Hong (Red River) of northern Vietnam by artistic farmers who became bored when the flood season put them out of work.

My next tourist attraction was the Water Puppet Theater in Hanoi (tickets are about three dollars for an hour performance). Puppeteers stand behind a screen in water up to their waists, controlling the puppets' movements with long bamboo poles. How they manipulate the puppets may not be a state secret, but certainly there are not many puppeteers advertising their techniques.

In the hour performance I watched 12 acts, each telling a story of myth about Vietnam and its history. There were stories about planting and harvesting rice, fishing, and boat races. What made the experience so enchanting was the colorful puppets in and above the water, traditional musicians playing a sound track to match the action, and singers who narrated the stories. It is a first class performance that has been seen around the world as Vietnam exports this unique form of art.

The puppet theatre seated fewer than a thousand people so everyone in the audience could feel an intimate part of the action and storytelling.

Two final notes on my holiday in Hanoi starts with a confession: I am weak of the flesh. American expatriates living in Asia subsist on more than noodles and rice. Every evening in Hanoi I visited Pizza 112 on Hang Bong Street to partake of cheeseburgers, pasta, pizza, and potato soup, which was better than mother used to make. One evening I met Giang, Mai, Tu, and Phuong. Tu was especially happy because the date was October 13 and that's her birthday. The high school students were there to celebrate in Italian fashion with pizza, sing their rendition of the birthday song, and shower gifts on Tu.

On my final day of touring I chanced upon Ngoc Khanh and her cousin, at Den Ngoc Son (Temple of the Jade Mound) on a tiny islet at Hanoi's Hoan Kiem Lake. When I asked why they were burning papers, their response was that they were giving gifts to the angels. Further conversation revealed that they were paying respects to their ancestors by burning paper houses, cars, and money, which then went up to the heavens in smoke. Ancestor worship is of high moral and social significance in Vietnamese society. Failure to honor one's ancestors is a serious matter that condemns the ancestor to a life of hellish wandering and subsisting on charity. Not good! In Singapore, the seventh lunar month (July-August) is devoted to ancestor worship. It is called the Hungry Ghost Festival.

The perennial problem in our good experiences is that they come to an end, we're sorry about that but still find inspiration in making plans to continue those fun ways in the future. Hanoi here I come (back)!

Acknowledgements

This is my second book of stories about experiences I've had with people and travel. There are also some opinions and truisms that came to me as a result of meeting people who made my life better. From the time we're born we are assimilating our surroundings as we pick and choose the values that others model for us. As kids we learn from other kids, our parents, ministers, teachers, friends, and family. My life was formulated by association with some incredibly fine people that I was fortunate enough to meet on my happy journey.

They taught me the importance of being involved in life by helping others, striving for improvement, and being positive in word and deed. This rather large crowd of helpful people has made a huge difference in my life by teaching me to be observant and appreciative for the gifts and talents that we all possess.

The 53 stories in *A Happy Journey* reflect experiences I had from 2004 through 2007, while I was working for the Naval Criminal Investigative Service in Singapore. My work involved completing vulnerability assessments at seaports and airports in 20 countries of the South Pacific, Oceana, and Asia. In all, I traveled to 110 locations to complete nearly 200 assessments that were subsequently used by fleet commanders in planning antiterrorism measures. In most of 2008, I was experiencing life as an English teacher in Thailand and there are stories about that, too.

In my official travels I was seldom by myself. There was usually at least one stalwart workmate that kept me focused on the work at hand, shared their good humor, and gave generously from a gift for gab. These superb personalities were Scott Bernat, Bob Blons, Tom Boungivino, Frank Boyd, Joe Brummond, Mike Bryant, Brian Curley, Mike Douglas, Kel Ide, Jeri Jones, Nate Knowles, Michelle Kramer, Chris Leaden, Dennis

Manning, Rich McFetrich, Tom Mockler, Chris Neal, Corbin Rinehart, Pia Roth, John Salazar, John Smallman, and Kevin Wagoner. My travel stories are from our shared experiences.

Moving around the world isn't easy; my journey has been less strenuous because of strong friendships that gave me the right kind of orientation. I am indebted to the following generous and knowledgeable personalities who taught me the rights and wrongs of life in their world: Kemariah Duraman, Brunei; Hyacinth Dmello, Bruno D'Souza, George Martin, Jahangir and Merion Telyarkhan, Keki Master, and Lonny Fernandes and son Hayston, India; Julia Ambarsari, Kristin Febrianti Caroline, Tom Daley, Lucky Santini, Netty Kacaribu, Ginny Rustandi, Budi Setyaning, Dewi "Shanty" Susantini Luh, Inggrids Collyns Lubis, and Kusrini "Rina" Endang Sri, Indonesia; Bruce Acker, Bob Tate and Phoebe Chan, Malaysia; Walter Etcheverry, Roger Girard and Bernard Lavel, New Caledonia; Felicia Fernandes and Jim Roberts, East Timor; Lemapu Wong, Samoa; Terry and Nora Leggett, Doris Bay, Mary Chen, Dr. Martha Lee, Rebekah Lee, Captain Annie Lim, Lai Li Lian, Dr. Robert Don, Shila Mohammed, and Ernest Chen, Singapore; Majid and Leena Awn and family, Jim Oxley, and Tee Sims, Sri Lanka; Supaporn "Su" Toluang and son Copter, Wanvisa Techo and family, Chamaiporn "Lek" Sompinta, Eiw Boontiwa and daughter Jubjang, Thamnian "Elle" Tool-ong, Dokrang "Frean" Traiking, Sirinan "Nan" Boonyo, and Tantimaphon "Emm" Jaichuen, Thailand; Andrew Manuele, Vanuatu; and Tran Thi Mong Chinh, Nguyen Thi Hong Van, Pham Choung Dai, Robb Etnyre, and John Milkiewicz, Vietnam. And thanks to the many unnamed taxi drivers, hotel receptionists, waitresses, and street vendors that I met along the way who shared one thing or another about their way-of-life.

I wouldn't be much without all the good that my friends have made of me. They have shaped my world, defined my values, and always been ready on the sidelines to lend a helping hand.

I've been helped in construction of this book by five friends who served as peer readers and reviewers. They offered ideas on what was right and made excellent suggestions for improvement. My great thanks to Toastmasters friends Martha Lee in Singapore, Ralph Compton in Virginia, and Fred Ferate in Texas for your enthused willingness to help out. Extraordinary thanks to my high school classmate Jackie Delaverdac DeMent in Michigan for her eagle-eyed attention to grammar and to Captain Kurt Hummeldorf, a friend from our travels together in Indonesia, East Timor, Papua New Guinea, and Bangladesh. I applaud all of you for the bursts of creative energy you sent my way.

Thanks to the strangers who became friends, the hundreds of people who looked out for my well being, and all those who cared enough to share something about their lives. Each time I was touched by these human hands I was educated and entertained, having my heart expanded in the process.

I've tried to demonstrate through these reflections that although we are obviously different in skin color, religious beliefs, economic circumstances, thinking patterns, and culture, we're all closely related in the human family. We share commonality in our good hearts and the love we contribute to those around us.

I am indebted to friends, family, and strangers who have kept me smiling and wondering, made me rich in experiences, and taught me the value of positive thinking. Indeed, everyone we meet is our teacher in contributing another piece to the complicated puzzle that comprises the human condition.

Lastly, thank you to my sister, Linda. Over the years our family has grown smaller with the passing of grandparents, parents, aunts and uncles. Now Linda and I along with a few others are the survivors. Linda's example as a matriarch is what every family should have to show the way in kindness, love, and patience. We are lucky to have her inner glow to show us the way!

Cover Design

Front cover photography: Five students from Suankularb Wittayalai Rangsit School, Pathumthani, Thailand, on a field trip to Chokchai Farm, Khorat. Shown left to right: Nijaporn "Toey" Petsang, Peamjit "Ke" Wattanakitsiri, Supapitch "Mean" Kittisarakul, Wanalee "Air" Subartsawad, and Wanutchaporn "Nutty" Unsamak. The photo was taken July 2, 2008 and served as the genesis for a photo essay entitled, *Thai Girl Power.*

Back cover: Photograph of author, Larry Welch.

Design and photography by the author.

Index

W-X-Y-Z